Inside the Rainbow

By James Medley

Illustrations by Harry Long

FIRSTHAND BOOKS

Inside the Rainbow is an original publication of FirstHand Books. This work has never before appeared in book form. Any similarity to actual persons or events is purely coincidental.

Published by:
FirstHand Books
310 Cedar Lane
Teaneck, NJ 07666

Cover illustration by Harry Long
Illustrations by Harry Long
Design and typography by Laura Allen
Production by Michael Lewis

ISBN: 0-943383-09-9

PRINTED IN CANADA

CONTENTS

❖ ❖ ❖

INTRODUCTION

❖ ❖ ❖

I received my first lesson in race relations when I was four or five years old. I came from a large family of very devout Catholics, aunts, and uncles galore. In our small home town of Owensboro, Kentucky, there was only one word for the black inhabitants. Though that word wasn't employed by my parents, I heard it repeatedly from the rest of the family, cousins, and nephews.

One day my mother and aunt took me to the grocery store. I remained in the car while they shopped. An immense black woman approached the car parked beside ours, burdened with two large sacks of groceries. Being an extroverted, friendly kind of kid, I spoke to her. "Hello, nigger," I said.

"I'll cut your black heart out!" the woman shouted at me. Her large, round face was contorted with hatred. I was terrified.

On the way home, I related the curious incident, and my aunt was astonished at my ignorance. "We don't call them that to their faces!" she exclaimed indignantly. To my mother, she asked, "How could he be so stupid, Edith?"

Fortunately, my parents moved to Florida, and away from the clan. Of course, the hypocrisy of religion fell shortly thereafter. Then during the civil rights struggle, the Sixties and Seventies, the rest of the so-called "American Values" collapsed under their own bigoted weight—nothing unusual in that. I learned a great deal about the ugly face of anti-Semitism, racism, and prejudice during the five years I was a member of the Communist Party, USA. That was my first exposure to a large group of highly principled, and idealistic Jewish people who became my best friends in Miami.

There is a French proverb which states, "At night, all cats are gray." That sums it up fairly well. But the ultimate summation, the solution to racial intolerance, is simply love. Love is the closest thing we can conceive of the divine, and sex is how humans express it. Love is a glorious celebration of the flesh—

regardless of what color that flesh may be. I would hope that whatever talent I possess may contribute to advancing that love across all the artificially devised ethnic and cultural barriers erected by a barbaric society.

In this age of the dreaded scourge, perhaps flesh and the word are best conjoined. The opinions of editors vary, some opting for pulling on rubbers at every occasion, often with comical results. I once had three naked men flee a burning house and dive into a nearby pond. When they started getting it on, magically, the editor produced condoms. Perhaps he dredged them from the cattails which grew alongside or from the muck in which they wallowed.

"These people are made up!" I wanted to scream at him. "They're only in my head, and they can't catch anything." But then I recalled a little character of mine named Butter. A cute, little mischievous imp, I had literally fallen in love with him. We had a stormy two week relationship until I married him off to that same editor. Butter wears rubbers now and I'm happy for him.

This book is dedicated to Harry Ziegler, my lover of thirty-five years. I also wish to thank those loyal friends whose support has been invaluable: Ted Reinholtz, John and Ted, Robert and David, Danny and Mike, Norman Shapiro, Vince Sharman, Danny Rodriguez, John Bates, and all the wonderful black men I have known. I have been blessed with the most supportive mother and father, brothers, and sisters it is possible to have.

James Medley
June 1, 1994

Many of the activities described in Inside the Rainbow *have long been considered dangerous, and in the light of the current AIDS crisis, they could prove lethal today. The author and the publishers do not recommend that the reader attempt to duplicate them.*

Ancient History

❖ ❖ ❖

My ancestors very probably had been owned by Jeff's distant kin. He knew it and I knew it. Now, I know all this should be treated as ancient history, something which happened so long ago it would best be forgotten. But that isn't the way of the south. . .

Ancient History

Why in the hell my home office insisted on having our annual sales meeting in Minneapolis during the winter was beyond me, but it's been that way every year. All the other sales reps joke about the hotels being too crowded during the one week of summer they get up here in Minnesota. But this bone-chilling weather is pretty rough on a guy from the south like me.

I didn't feel so much like a square basketball on this trip as I did that first year after they recruited me out of college. For one thing, there are quite a few more black salesmen now. When I'd started, I was one of the first. Now I only had to contend with all these straight guys and their wives at the family functions which this progressive company sponsors.

On the first night, the brass threw a big, get-acquainted party at the fancy downtown hotel where we were staying. All our white-label name tags were ready for us at the door. My standard uniform—dark pinstripe suit, blue shirt, and red tie—was duplicated dozens of times by practically every other sales rep there. The women were decked out like colorful flowers in the bouquets we formed as we stood around talking together in clusters. I'd gotten over the "single" stigma pretty early on and made quite a few acquaintances, if not exactly friends, among my associates.

I was with two of these men whose territories adjoined mine in

Alabama and Mississippi. Mine was the state of Louisiana, where I was born. The regional sales manager, whom everyone calls Ace, approached our group with a single, youngish man in tow. He obviously wasn't a kid; he was in his early twenties, but he had a baby face on him. He was a good six feet tall, with fairly short hair that looked almost golden under the bright chandeliers of the ballroom. He was wearing the standard uniform. Though it's not written in the policy, I know this company hires for looks. And this kid would be a real charmer.

"Guys," Ace announced as he brought the young man into our circle. "This is Jeff, our new Texas rep." Jeff had a warm expression on his face and his cheeks had small dimples when he smiled. His eyes were a robin's egg blue. Ace began to introduce us. I had already spotted the kid's name tag, so when he got around to saying my name, "Charlie Canfield, meet Jeff Canfield," I was more prepared for it than the boss. He paused for just a second, as if for the first time realizing that we had the same last name.

Ace acted a little awkward, looking back and forth between us. Now, if we had been two white guys, he would normally have asked if we were related. But between my dark brown skin and Jeff's creamy tan, it was obvious we weren't. Ace recovered quickly enough (he was too polished to let his thinking show, as a good salesman must be), and continued. "So, anyway, Jeff, this is part of our southern force," he said, and left our group and hurried off.

Jeff didn't have any wife along with him, but the six of us stood around making small talk about the company, families, and all that other breeder stuff. One of the wives asked Jeff where he was from. Jeff told her Louisiana. "Why, what a coincidence," the woman said. "So is Charlie."

Jeff and I looked at one another, and each knew what the other was thinking. When she went on inquiring what part of the state we were both from, an electric wire of tension shot between us. We were both from Plaquemines Parish.

Now, I should probably explain that these other two couples had come to this sales meeting from up north, and wouldn't have understood what transpired between Jeff and myself at that moment. But we both knew our history pretty well, and knew the forgotten customs of the old south.

After the Civil War and the Emancipation, it was not uncommon for the slaves on any particular plantation to adopt the surname of their owner when they became free. So, the thought going through my head, and obviously Jeff's as well, was that my ancestors very probably had been owned by Jeff's distant kin. He knew it and I knew it. Now, I know all this should be treated as ancient history, something which happened so long ago it would best be forgotten. But that isn't the way of the south, where history has a nasty way of cropping up even in this day and age. "Sins of the fathers—" and all that.

I gracefully excused myself from the group and made for the open bar where I ordered another Chivas and water. I cursed myself for that damned resentment which welled up in my chest. It was unreasonable, I knew; I had a Master's degree from Tulane. I was a very successful salesman, given the top sales award for the last three years running, and was well liked and respected in my territory. I owned my own house in New Orleans, had plenty of friends. The only vacuum in my life was a lover, but I'd pretty well adjusted to that after I'd been through two: one white, one black.

When Jeff ambled over beside me at the bar, I can't say that I didn't feel a little bristly—again, irrationally. "Buy you a drink?" he asked in a friendly way.

"They're free," I said abruptly.

"Oh, yeah," he stammered. "I forgot."

I felt a little shitty about my attitude, so I asked him what he was having. "Same as you," he replied immediately. Which for some reason, pissed me off even more; he didn't even know what I was drinking, and I took his remark for condescension.

"Scotch and water," I told the bartender. He poured some rotgut from the well into a plastic glass and handed it to me. I passed it back to Jeff.

"Thanks," he said, taking it from me and inclining his head. He almost choked on the first swallow, but he didn't say anything. I knew it was ridiculous, but his silence angered me as well. You couldn't have paid me to drink that shit, but he didn't protest, thinking it was what I liked. I felt like he was patronizing me.

"What high school did you go to?" Jeff asked, his tone lightly conversational.

I told him where I went and he told me where he went and there was the damned gap again. Our respective schools had been, for the most part, racially divided. Absolutely the only thing we had in common, outside of that hallowed ancestry, was our job. So we got on well enough discussing that and avoiding the personal stuff. Jeff excused himself to go to the bathroom, and as he returned across the crowded room, I couldn't help noticing how good-looking he was. Though he was a touch shorter than I, you could see he had a good tight body by the way he moved. I felt a stirring in my groin as his leg accidentally brushed against mine when he slid in beside me at the bar.

I'd had about enough of this breeder intensive atmosphere for the night, so I began to make preliminary excuses to leave.

"Want me to get a bottle?" Jeff asked. "We could have a nightcap in my room. We're the only homeboys way up here and far from home."

"Homeboys, huh?" I said, and left it at that. The damned rancor again. But he'd reminded me how far away from home I really was. So I relented and agreed to have a drink in his room. "But I'm buying the bottle." The package store in the lobby was still open and I bought a liter of Chivas. Jeff didn't say anything but looked kind of curiously at me.

Jeff's room had a round glass table with two chairs in front of the window, and we sat there after he'd fixed us each a drink. He didn't choke on the first swallow, but he didn't comment on the change of brands either. We'd both slung our jackets on the bed and loosened our ties and collars. Jeff had unbuttoned his shirt midway, and I could see his smooth and yellow-furred pecs, his frame as solid and compact as a high school track star.

I sat there a few moments, a bit uncomfortable, thinking about the vagaries of life. Here were two guys in the same strange hotel, thousands of miles from what was home to each of them, working for the same company in the same job, even sharing the same last name. Why, we should have been the closest buddies imaginable, damned near brothers. And yet, that fucking thing was there.

"You seem a little distant, Charlie," Jeff said, as he swirled his glass in circles on the glass table.

"Yeah. Well," I muttered.

"Yeah, I know," he said. "Me too." He was silent for several minutes. "Fucking life," he half-whispered, then said nothing more.

I took a hefty swig of my drink, a deep breath. "Maybe this wasn't such a good idea, Jeff. I'd better go."

"Please don't, Charlie," he said in an intimate way. "Can't we talk? I mean, really talk?"

"Rather not," I said, knocking back the rest of the Scotch. Immediately he took the empty glass from me, snatched his up, and hurried to the dresser where the ice cubes were. He looked sort of desperate as he refilled our drinks.

"There was never any segregation in the bedroom, you know," he said slipping into the chair across from me.

"So?" I muttered, and let it stand.

"So, maybe my great, great granddaddy—like, uh, well—knew some of your family."

"Knew?" I said, and I laughed. "You mean fucked." I was being deliberately cruel now and Jeff was fairly wallowing in it.

"C'mon, man," he said earnestly. "You know what I mean."

"Sure I do," I said in an aggrieved tone. "Big man from the white house sneaks down to the nigger shacks every night and gets some poontang better'n his old lady."

"Lighten up, man. It's not our fault."

That made me feel like a total idiot and I was madder at myself than I was at him. I said, "I'm sorry," though I wasn't exactly sure what I was apologizing for.

"I'm sorry too," Jeff said, and I think I did know what he was apologizing for.

We sat there in complete silence, each avoiding the other's gaze. And then, all of a sudden, we both burst out laughing. From then on, I can hardly explain what happened. But we each impulsively reached across the table and grabbed each other by the arms. And held on.

And held on.

And held on, too long for it to be simply relief. I felt the bunched muscles of Jeff's biceps as he squeezed mine, flexing and striated, felt something else as he kneaded my shoulders, felt more when his fingers lightly brushed my neck, a soft caress. At this close range, I noticed that his bright blue eyes had flecks of gold in them. And they were speaking volumes to my fervid ones. My cock started snaking out the leg of my Calvins and crawling down my thigh, leaving a wet trail and pushing at my dress pants.

One glance through the glass-topped table was enough to see that the folded lump in Jeff's crotch was swelling to a big-headed boner. Our eyes locked together as he raised his from staring at my obvious erection. The smile which drew Jeff's dimples into an impish grin melted the Minnesota night.

And then, without a word, we jumped up and were all over each other in less time than it takes to tell it. Jeff's lips were soft and moist as he covered my mouth with his own. My hands dug into his smallish buttocks and found them firm and perfectly round. He pressed his groin into mine, and I could feel his hardness and heat through our pants. We clawed frantically at one another, and our embrace was that of reunited lovers, clinging fast to each other and grinding our sex together.

Jeff instinctively realized I wouldn't take offense when he said, "You have a mind to get a little of your own back?"

I chuckled at that and said, "Yeah, honky, I do," hoping it came off in the same spirit.

Jeff unknotted my tie and began unbuttoning my shirt. His soft hands fluttered like butterflies as he shoved the shirt back off my shoulders and played with my stiffening nipples. I have quite a patch of wiry hair in a straight line across my chest, then nothing but smooth dusky skin till it hits my luxuriant pubic bush. Jeff's hand dived straight into my pants and clutched my hardening cock. His fingers formed a funnel over the head and he worked them greasily down the upright shaft.

I started undressing him. He wore the same Calvin Klein underwear that I did. The white fabric stood out in almost as much relief against his darkly tanned body as it did against my chocolate skin. I wasn't in all that much hurry to get the briefs off; they looked so good on him. His cock lay long and hard in the valley of his groin, jutting to the very edge of his muscular flanks. His underwear showed a darker patch of oozing lube. Oddly enough, the blond hair on his chest duplicated mine in that same straight pattern across his well-formed pecs, leaving his flat belly bare till it hit the deep "V" of his groin. Everything I'd felt about Jeff earlier washed away as he stood appraising my body.

"Damn, but you're a beautiful man, Charlie," he said. He stood a little way back and began touching me all over. He ran his palms over my nipples and cupped my pecs, then he trailed down the cleavage of my chest. He toyed with my navel, avoiding my straining cock in a teasing way and gliding over my loins to between my legs. His hands moved up and down softly on the inside of my thighs, every light touch of his fingers sending tingles of pleasure along my exquisitely tactile nerves.

Jeff was kissing my ears when he suddenly stopped. "Well, I'll be—go to hell," he exclaimed, examining behind my right ear. "You've got a little birthmark just like me." He pulled his ear away from the side of his face, and sure enough, there was the same little imperfect triangle that I had, though mine was whitish on the dark and his was the reverse. I didn't respond.

We fell onto the bed and grappled with one another, kicking our suits to the floor. I loved Jeff in just his underwear, not yet naked. I loved feeling all over his swollen pouch and kneading up between his cheeks through the material. I tortured myself with anticipation of the stiff treasure stored inside, feeling the heat of his hard cock under the thin white cotton, feeling the smooth round globes of his ass. We tongue-fucked each other's mouth. He sucked his way around my lips, drawing an oval with his head as he sucked them hard from the upper to the lower. Then he was back onto my tongue, sucking it out of my mouth as if it were a cock. Slobber ran between us and we ground our bodies together.

I propelled Jeff to his back and his head came up and he dove his soft, wet mouth into my armpit. His quivering tongue slathered spit over my wiry hair till it was soaked and trailing. Then the other. I stiff-armed myself above him and fed him nipples. He nipped with his teeth and sucked till they were hard and standing out on my chest like Hershey's Kisses. He grabbed my hips and dragged my leaking cock across his belly, between his hardened pecs and to his face. There, he finally pulled my underwear down.

"So beautiful. So beautiful," he murmured over and over, wondrously stroking my long black cock and licking on the uncut head. He skinned back my dick, held it up straight, and ran the thick, underside tube through his dripping lips, nuzzling into my low-hanging balls and slurping noisily between my splayed-open legs. I spread them further.

I reached beneath our writhing torsos and pushed his underwear down to just below his ass and groin. His cock was wet with pre-cum, and I smeared up the shank and jacked him slowly. His dick-skin was like heated velvet.

I lifted one leg just enough to struggle out of the now confining underwear and straddled his face again. Then I scrunched my hips further to his brow and framed his face with my ass. I felt his first tentative tongue swipes up my crack, his teasing nibbles at my hole. Jeff went for the kiss more delectable than any other. His soft lips locked onto my ass-mouth and he started spearing his tongue inside me. The long, deep strokes he used caused me to tremble and sent rippling sensations of ecstasy up and down my spine. I arched backward and jacked both our cocks slowly while he ate me out. Little contented murmurs escaped from his buried face. But I was getting too close to coming, with him just eating me that way.

I pulled off his face and slid wetly down his body, dragging down his drawers with my foot the rest of the way. He kicked them off his ankles. Now our sex-flesh was united. The glorious feel of naked meat, grinding against one another. We dispelled another old notion then: his cock was bigger than mine, more than an inch longer than my respectable length. And it was a little fatter as well.

I wanted to taste his cock so I scrambled backward and got between his lightly tufted legs. I held his dick rigidly aloft and licked all over the swollen head, tasting his mellow pre-cum on my tongue. My ample lips engulfed his root, and I felt every throbbing vein within the softness of his skin, so fast upon the hardness of his boner. Ecstatically, I sucked his joint and Jeff sighed and moaned pleasurably above me. I wanted to drink his sweet young load, but I wanted to fuck him too. My dick won out in the end.

I reared back on my haunches and pushed Jeff's legs in the air, bent him near double with his ass in my face. His cheeks were taut and firm, vibrant as I stroked the smoothest part of his flesh. I palmed his asscheeks apart and wedged my head into his crack. A tart and bittersweet taste met my tongue as I laved up and down Jeff's crack, washing over his pucker which felt hotter than the rest of him. Drawing concentric circles to his sweet little nether mouth, I slid my tongue inside him. He moaned and I jabbed straight in with furious little thrusts. I gnawed inside his hole and smothered his ass-lips with my feeding mouth.

Jeff jacked wildly on his cock, swinging above his face. I pawed at his balls and held the base of his shaft while he pumped madly on the meat extending from my fist. I joined my hand with his and we set up a quick stroking rhythm on his slippery bone that both our hands barely covered.

Then I stopped jacking him and slipped my hands up over his rump, up his jerking thighs and over the calves to his ankles. I held his legs spread in the air and climbed up his backside with my groin rutting tightly to his sweating flesh. Not guiding it, I brought my leaking tool to his wet, hot hole with hunches of my hips.

I nudged my flaring head against his pucker and felt his tight hole spreading my cum-slit open. His rosebud sheathed my glans, and I felt my foreskin sliding back onto the pulsing shaft, and the purple knob unhooding inside his assflesh as it entered him. The beautiful contrast of black and white sex-skin was a real turn-on for me.

"Easy, man. Go easy," Jeff moaned. "Fuck me slow."

Exactly what I had in mind: a good, long and drawn-out man-fuck. "Yeah," I mumbled thickly. "Gonna fuck you slow, man. Slow and dirty. Gonna give you a good, slow, down-and-nasty dirty-fuck."

I fed him a little more sausage, then paused and held the head tight inside him while I muscle-jerked my cock till he got used to its girth filling him. I gyrated my hips a little, scouring his ass-walls and burrowing deeper into his tunnel. Then I pulled back, held my cock fast at his pucker, lubing up and making sure he was staying open. I plowed the same field, getting in a little further with each renewed drive. An inch, another, one more. He was beginning to take it good now, his satiny assflesh spreading open before my advancing rod. My knob was like a club, battering its way into his guts.

I felt his soft and warm fuck-channel spread apart like the sweetest cock-hole I'd ever gotten my dick inside, yielding like a rich pudding. Jeff clenched his teeth, bit his lower lip, and thrashed his head from side to side as I drove relentlessly up his chute. I bored into him with one mighty thrust, and he gasped but didn't cry out.

I rutted hard against his coccyx and ground my pelvic bone against him, grinding out the fuck of my life.

"Ah shit! God, sweet Jesus!" he panted when I was in him all the way to my balls. "Fuck me, Charlie! Fuck the cum outta me!"

I put all my weight in my midsection, lifted my legs from the bed, and literally rode on his ass, my arms straight-armed to each side of his head. He was bent double now, his cock approaching his face.

"Suck it, man!" I grunted. "Suck that fucking dick!"

Then I started pounding away inside him, plunging in and out, driving his dick down his throat. I bucked on him like a bronco and shoved his meat over halfway in. Tears ran in streams from his eyes. His slobber splashed out of his cock-stuffed mouth. His cheeks were red and bulging with his own cock. I pistoned in him like a racing engine, and got more of his meat inside his bulging throat. I was in him so deep, it felt like my dick was down there too.

Then I went into a spiking, slamming, all-out fuck, and all he could do was gag, gasp and groan around his embedded slab of cockflesh. My legs still lifted, I wriggled and squirmed atop him, just my dick and ass moving rapidly as I punched in mightily and wallowed in him like a fucking dog.

"Getting my own back," he'd said. Yes, and with a vengeance. I went pig-crazy in his ass, deep-dicking frenziedly like I wanted to fuck him into the next county. The mists of the past swirled through my head like flying leaves in the wind. No one in the world now but the two of us, atoning, making up in love for all the hate. I wanted to come deep in this man, wanted him to come inside himself. Cum, as a balm to soothe that hurt, all those years and that one thing between us. Cock and cum.

"Jeff! Jeff! Jeff!" I panted again and again, matching every gasp with a brutal lunge which jabbed my cockhead savagely against his trigger. "Milk me, baby! Oh, God! I'm gonna come!"

Jeff reached around my pumping ass and dug his hands into my cheeks, viciously drawing my cock in and out of him. He fingered my hole. My nuts drew up in their sac. A jolting ejaculation began to swell between my legs, electrical pricks darting through my creambag, balls buzzing. Pile driving, I fucked him. He was gagging on his cock and he quaked and trembled like an animal in the throes of a fit.

I started slapping his asscheeks with all my strength. "Come! Come! Come, you fucker, Come!" It felt like some spirit overtook me and I wanted to flog him, flail every patch of his white skin till it was red and stinging. It was as if I'd lost my mind, become a sex-starved maniac. Then his eyes went wild, rolled back in his head, and came back snapping with fire. He looked possessed by a feral demon, intoxicated with sex and lustful wantonness, craving to be fucked to death.

Jeff began to pummel my back with flailing fists, furious slapping lashes which magnified mine. We beat on each other, locked in lust and blood and cum. His blood in my veins, filling the sword of love I impaled him with. We battered on each other with the distant past, a swampy dream of humid nights and wretched cabins, cries of a strangled lust filling the dark, close quarters.

"Fuck that ass! Fuck that ass! Fuck that ass!" I grunted gutturally.

From Jeff came wild strangled moans.

And the gravy gushed out of me like an opened hydrant. With a wild scream, I let it loose. And my jizz shot out like a pent-up river, flushing my balls and draining what felt like my core and essence. The muscles of my ass jumped and trembled, my body quaking under the tremendous onslaught of a jolting stream of juice as my dick honey flooded into Jeff.

His throat muscles were rippling and gobbling on his own spewing spunk. I could actually see the cum as it raced along his downside tube and gushed his glory down his throat. Jism poured from his lips as he tried to contain it all, but didn't succeed. Silver streams ran down his cheeks and dribbled onto his chin.

The smells of sex and sweat and cum were overpowering, and I gave myself over to the most satisfying fuck I'd ever had. The pleasure was so intense, it was nearly painful. He drained me empty of my seed, milking my cock with experienced strokes of his well-fucked ass. We shuddered and quaked to a deathly stillness. I pulled out of his hole and collapsed exhausted beside him, heaving and gasping for air.

"Good God, Charlie!" he panted as he unbent himself and stretched full length next to me. "What the fuck happened just then?"

I turned my head sideways to him and rolled his face closer to mine. "Not being a superstitious guy, " I whispered, "I'd have to say it was chemistry."

During the night, we made long and languorous love and he fucked me tenderly. We exchanged addresses before the meeting broke up.

Back in New Orleans, I went to visit my grandfather who still lived in the French Quarter. He was sitting on his balcony, shirtless, as the day was hot. I was struck immediately by the graying hair in a straight line across his chest, just as my father's had been. Just like Jeff's.

"Tell me some more about our family's past," I asked him after the pleasantries were attended to.

"Ancient history, son," he said resignedly. "Let's just get on with today." He turned his head away and looked out into the distance where the Mississippi River curved around a bend. In the rich light of the setting sun, I saw the little white birthmark behind his ear. "Just got to get on with today," he repeated thoughtfully.

Which is exactly what I plan to do when I meet Jeff at his place the next time. There's nothing like loving your half-brother, a few generations removed.

Tough Love

❖ ❖ ❖

It was as if Johnny had become another person. All of a sudden, he was acting meek and bashful. I would never have believed it if I hadn't seen it with my own eyes. The black man advanced to Johnny and groped his swollen hard-on.

Tough Love

Johnny Gash was an ornery son of a bitch, as hateful as his name, mean as a junkyard dog, nastier than cat shit, and so forth. He'd been held back twice, so he'd turned twenty during our senior year. His face resembled two miles of bad road, scowling all the time. Between the acne craters and a scar which tore through his left eyebrow like a streak of lightning, he looked like a young gangster. Even nowadays, he still wears a greasy ducktail. His hair is as black as his temper. Back then, he was mad at the world, a chip on his shoulder so big, you could make two-by-fours out of it. But you get the idea; every school has one.

I'll have to confess right at the outset that I've been called a nerd. My optometrist says I can't wear contacts so I'm stuck with these Coke-bottle glasses. But I've also been told that when I take them off I do have beautiful blue eyes. And my body's in pretty good shape since I swim a lot in the lake down the street from our house. And my hair is bleached blond by the Florida sun.

But back to Johnny. He'd been bullying me ever since middle school. When I was much younger, he would waylay me in the alley we both used to walk to school. If I'd been old enough to file income tax, I could've used him as a deduction, so much lunch money had I parted with. It got so he would walk up to me and hold out his hand. I felt like a wimp, but I handed it over every time. He'd stuff it in his pants and walk off without saying boot, shoot, or scoot to me. I was grateful when they put him in reform school for six months.

I don't consider myself a sissy, although I've known I was gay since...well, for a long time. The first time Johnny picked on me, I'd fought like a tiger against him. Didn't do any good. He beat the living shit out of me. Literally. It was one of the worst days of my life. So I'd given up scrapping with him and gave in to his greedy requests.

But something happened in Johnny's and my adversarial relationship last week that bothered me a lot. I thought Johnny was still at the reform school which everybody refers to as the farm. I had been to the only downtown movie here in our small hometown and was walking home by myself around midnight. Sometimes there was some action in the balcony or the bathrooms, but there hadn't been any that night and I was as horny as a goat. The street lights shone dimly through the overhanging canopy of live oak trees. I turned a corner which was obscured by a tall cherry hedge and ran right smack into Johnny Gash.

We collided and it scared the yell out of me. I did yell.

"Well if it ain't punk Cory," Johnny said. He wore a grin like an open razor. "Does your mommy know her little boy's out so late?" His liquored-up breath had the force of a knockout punch.

I recoiled. "When did they let you out? What do you want, Johnny?" I asked resignedly.

"Somethin' hot to stick my dick in," he answered with a snarl that frightened the bejesus out of me. "Like some little cocksucker's mouth."

I ignored him and meekly said, "I've got four bucks left over from the movie—how about that?"

"I'll take that too," he slurred. "Follow me."

"I've gotta get home, Johnny," I pleaded. "C'mon, get out of the way."

"Guess you still ain't learned your lesson, huh? Gotta get rough with you. Is that what you want, huh? Want me to beat your punk little ass again?"

"I'm not looking for any trouble, Johnny. Here, take the money." I dug the wadded bills out of my worn out jeans, and he snatched them from my hand like a hungry heron. "Now let me go."

"I know you want to, Cory," he whispered drunkenly. "Known you been wantin' ta suck on this big old cock for years." He groped himself in an obscene way, squeezing his fat fucker down the leg of his pants and outlining the bloated shaft against the rubbed-raw denim. I couldn't take my eyes off the godawful thing.

"Yeah, that's it boy, look at it. See how big my fucker is. Feel it."

"I ain't gonna suck your cock, Johnny," I replied, falling into his atrocious manner of speaking.

"Just look at that purty little mouth you got. It'll wrap aroun' this old hog-cock jest right. Now let's quit foolin' roun' and get it over with. You gonna to do it anyhow."

I didn't know who I was the most mad at, Johnny or my cock. Because I'd thrown a boner that he couldn't have missed if he'd been wearing a mask. My teenage sap was racing to my groin and swelling up my dick with enough blood to make me pass out from loss to the brain, not to mention that my heart was pounding loudly enough for a deaf man to hear it.

Johnny grabbed my wrist and shoved my hand onto his stiff rod. The smell of liquor on his breath was practically as overpowering as the weakness I felt in my knees, which threatened to buckle any second.

"Rub it, Cory. It itches real bad," Johnny huskily growled. "I was pissing in the woods yesterday and a bee stung my dick. It's swoll up real bad, and the more you rub it the harder it gits and the worse it itches and then you got to rub it more and it gits even harder and so on till it's damned near hurtin' me. I need to git some slobber on it to soothe it out some. If I come, maybe it'll go down."

With goosebumps on my arms and trembling legs, I stroked Johnny's cock.

"Ah yeah, that feels good man, real good," he murmured, almost gentle.

"You got a place we can go?" I asked, painfully conscious of being right out on the street, even if it was after midnight.

"I tole you to follow me," Johnny said. "C'mon."

If anybody in town had seen Johnny and me walking side by side, they would have blabbed it all over. Our mutual antagonism was well known about town. I'd been the brunt of too many locker room jokes to think about it. But I meekly let him lead me down three blocks and then turn in the direction of his house. Surely we wouldn't go there. If anything, Johnny's parents are worse than he is, about the meanest bunch of redneck rattlesnakes hereabouts. But under the soft yellow light of the moon, I could see we were headed for a vacant lot with a broken-down shack sitting in the rear under a huge chinaberry tree.

I was as nervous as I've ever been in my life, isolated and with not a house for as far as you could see, I would be completely at Johnny's mercy. What if he decided to really whip my butt after I'd blown him? Nobody would be able to hear me screaming, and even if they did, he could say I was trying to put the make on him and he hated queers. I saw no way out of my predicament.

Johnny pushed me through the door, and it was black dark in there, darker still as he slammed the door behind us. He felt around in the dark, finally locating and lighting a single candle which he set onto an upended orange crate. By its feeble light, I saw there was little else in the tight space but a bare, worn out mattress.

"Strip," Johnny gruffly commanded. "I wanna see how hard you get with my cock in your purty little mouth."

He proceeded to shuck out of his coveralls. He wore Jockey shorts that were stained with piss and cum all over the front. Salaciously he groped his hard-on through them, and lube-drool spread a new patch of wetness on the thin white fabric. Then he stripped them off and threw them at me. They hit me in the face and I smelled his funkiness—not half bad. Before I threw them off, I got a couple of deep whiffs of Johnny's virile maleness. I had never seen Johnny naked before, but when I did, I was sorry I hadn't earlier.

As burly, rough, and ugly as his face was, his body was the opposite. He was thin-hipped and lanky, a little beer gut starting to show just above his tapered groin. His fat cock was indeed swollen and red. He was uncut, and his dickflesh hung like a nozzle over the fat knob. I don't know how he maintained the muscular firmness of his torso, for I'd never seen him do any work at all. His pecs were nicely clefted and taut, and there was a glistening tone to the muscles of his arms.

He got his heavy fucker in his fist and pointed it at me like a weapon. "See where that motherfucker stung me," he said, punching out his hips and pointing to the bloated head. I could see an angry crimson patch just under the deep flange of his crown. It bulged out the side and made his cock look like a monstrous club.

"In for a penny, in for a pound," I thought as I dropped my jeans. My cock was raring at the fly of my Calvins, threatening to slip up and out of the waistband. Johnny took two steps toward me and pushed me forcefully back onto the stained mattress. It was stiff and rough and smelled like buckets of shot-off cum.

Then he spread his legs apart and dragged my head up to his

crotch. His funk struck me worse than his liquored-up breath had. Johnny wagged that swollen cock-knob right in front of my eyes. He started slapping my cheeks with it. My cock succeeded in freeing itself. It leapt to attention and saluted my navel, drooling lube-juice and wetting up my flat belly. I hate to admit it, but Johnny's swaggering domination of me was beginning to turn me on.

"Now suck that fucking dick, you little cocksucking queer!" he panted, shoving it up to my lips.

That barked command got me even hotter. I admitted I was enjoying the humiliation. With the fat head that close to my eyes, I could see that the bee's stinger was still embedded in the soft folds of cockflesh.

"Why you old tomfool," I said, "no wonder it hurts, you ain't pulled the stinger out yet."

"Suck it out," he said in a raspy voice.

Pre-cum was seeping out of his cock-nozzle and dripping down in a clear strand a good five inches. I slurped it up with my tongue before it thinned out at the top and fell. It tasted mellow and sweet to my palate. Then I got the skin-curtain in my lips and sucked where the stinger was. It slid out easily and I maneuvered it around in my mouth till I caught it between my teeth and bared them so Johnny could see it. Then I bit it in half and swallowed.

"Kneel down on the floor, faggot," he harshly slurred. "I gotta piss."

Nothing like that had ever happened to me before, but I did as he ordered. Feeling like a whipped cur, I got on all fours and he stood over me. It took him awhile to get his piss spraying, but when he did, he flushed out a horse-piss that ran in streaming yellow rivers all over me. I turned my face up to him and he hosed a jet-stream of warm urine down my throat. I drank every drop.

Then he walked around me, still gushing urine on my back, and yanked down my underwear to my thighs, ripping them to shreds till there was just ragged fabric hanging between my legs. When he started washing my ass-ditch with his hot liquid, I thought I was going to shoot off. Johnny hunkered into a half squat and sprayed his thick stream of pee onto my hanging balls. The force was so strong, they swayed in their bag like a sack of tomatoes. My torn Calvins were wringing wet. Finished, he commanded me to get back on the bed. I did.

I went back onto Johnny's meat and succeeded in getting the

gummy knob between my lips. His piss tasted salty and pungent. I forced as much of his rod down my gullet as I could till my cheeks bloated with the effort. I pushed a rolling wave of dickflesh before my advancing lips and his soft foreskin swaddled my mouth as I engulfed all his big organ down my throat.

Johnny started moving his hips and groaning, throat-fucking me in a rutting frenzy. No preliminaries for this dude, just grab a cum-catcher off the street and get off in his mouth. I was the designated catcher. And I was loving it.

"Ah yeah! Shit!" he grunted, picking up a quicker rhythm and spearing his heavy fucker in wild abandon. Sometimes he'd even miss my throat and the fat knob would jab out the side of my mouth, grinding out my cheeks. "Suck that fucking dick! Suck it! Suck it!"

I sucked. And I sucked. And sucked. And he frenziedly face-fucked me with no tenderness or compassion. Johnny grabbed the back of my bobbing head and ferociously pulled me onto his hog-cock, like he was jacking off with my face.

"Take my load, man—here it comes!" he yelped. He started blasting off down my throat, and his cock jerked like a discharging pistol down my gullet. Great gushers of jizz flooded my mouth and I gagged on the spewing spunk.

Then, for the first time in my life, I realized I was coming too, without even touching myself. Hot spits of dick-honey bathed my belly and spurted onto my chest from my hard cock, harder than I ever remembered it being. I held it forcefully down and sprayed it onto what was left of my dripping, piss-soaked underwear. I geysered off four or five ropy streams until my cock started drooling more juice which bathed the head in my seed. I don't remember ever shooting so much creamy milk. It mixed with the running piss and pooled in my navel.

"Liked sucking cum, didn't ya, cocksucker?" Johnny snarled, squeezing out the last drops of his juice and flinging them in my face by whipping his dick smartly up and down. "Liked being pissed on too, right?"

Before I could assent or even clean the cum off my belly, we heard a light tapping at the door. Johnny's head jerked around at the sound. He skinned into his piss-stained underwear in a flash and motioned for me to be still. That was unnecessary because I was already scrabbling around the bare mattress and trying to collect my clothes. I succeeded in getting the tattered remnants of my underwear half concealing my crotch.

I saw the door start to open and Johnny made a dash for it. He caught it before the intruder got his head inside.

"Not now," I heard him say. His voice cracked with nervousness. Then he disappeared out the door, closing it behind him. I held my Calvins together as best I could and crept to the crack of the door-jamb.

I heard Johnny whispering in a desperate way. "I can't, man, not now. I'm busy doing homework."

Then I heard a strange gravelly voice mutter insistently, "I saw the light through the crack, knew you'd be in there. C'mon, Johnny. It won't take but a minute. Let me fuck you again. I really need to get my ashes hauled."

"Ssshhh!" I heard Johnny whisper. "It's late. Somebody will find my hiding place."

"You got somebody in there, Johnny? Why can't I come in? You trying to hide pussy from me, maybe some boy-pussy like we had on the farm? Huh?"

"No! I tole you I was studying. Now git."

"You ain't never studied a day in your life, Johnny Gash. Why're you shitting me?"

I heard the stranger trying to open the door and Johnny scuffling with him. When the burly young man succeeded in getting through the door, I could see why Johnny hadn't stood a chance of keeping him out.

I had never seen the young stranger around town before, and I was certain if I had seen him I would've remembered.

He was around six-feet-five, maybe taller. His arms were like hams, and his broad black face was pleasant and handsome. His lips were full and fleshy, a blackberry purple. And his crotch looked like he'd stepped from a Tom of Finland drawing. The folded lump at his groin bulged out the khaki pants he wore as if he had a fat sausage stuck down there. He wore a baseball cap backward on his head.

"Well now, ain't this something," he said. "Old Johnny's got another sweetheart, a little boy-cunt. Trying to keep 'im all to himself."

I was still standing there in my piss-soaked and ripped up underwear, and this handsome stud stripped them off me with his eyes. Johnny stood behind him with an agonized expression on his face.

"Did he fuck you yet, Johnny? Get his cock up your ass like you're always hankering for?" the man swiveled his head and asked.

Johnny's whole body turned as red as his bee-stung dick.

The man returned his attention to me. "How about it, kid, did you give Johnny a deep-dicking fuck?"

I shook my head no.

"Well, why the hell not?" he asked. "That's all the little fucker liked in reform school."

I grinned at Johnny and his cock got hard. This stranger felt like an ally. His sudden presence, and Johnny's equally sudden change in demeanor, emboldened me.

"Let me watch you do it," I said to the black man. "I'll hold him down and you fuck him."

It was as if Johnny had become another person. All of a sudden, he was acting meek and bashful. I would never have believed it if I hadn't seen it with my own eyes. The black man advanced to Johnny and groped his swollen hard-on. Johnny looked helplessly at me as the man pulled off his briefs. Then he stripped.

"I just came, Earl. I can't do it no more," Johnny whined.

Looking at that monster fucker swinging between Earl's beefy thighs, I didn't see how he'd ever gotten it up Johnny's bunghole in the first place. But apparently they had done it pretty often because Earl said, "Your cock's hard now just thinking about it. You'll shoot again when I get it in you. Get on the bed."

Johnny did as he was told, going straight to the mattress and flopping down on his belly like an obedient puppy.

Earl looked at me and said, "C'mon, kid, I want you to lick it in 'im."

Earl crawled onto the mattress and straddled Johnny's thighs. His gleaming black ass was awesome. His dark, glistening prick was even more awe inspiring. Against Johnny's smooth white ass-globes, it looked even bigger, like a misshapen eggplant. I kneeled on the bed beside them and watched as Earl rode his fuckstick up and down Johnny's crack, wetting him up with leaking lube-juice.

"Lick on it boy," Earl said in a lewd, seductive whisper. "Juice it up for his tight ass."

I bent over in a crouch and tried to suck Earl's cock. I could barely get the huge head inside, and it bulged out my neck when I managed to get half of it in my throat.

"That's it, boy," Earl grunted. "Suck that meat so I can fuck

Johnny good. " He played with my ass and fondled my dripping cock and balls as I slurped and slobbered his tool through my lips. Then Earl pulled my head off his cock and throatily moaned, "Spit in his ass, juice'im up."

I did better than that. Again, I would never have believed that I actually got a liplock on Johnny's funky asscrack and ate him out. His musky stink was intoxicating, and I licked and laved his pucker till he was running with spit. I gave him darting tongue-stabs up his hole, and his bittersweet essence was overpowering.

Johnny moaned and sighed. Earl spread Johnny's legs wide apart. Then he lay on top of Johnny and spread his on top of them.

"Now get between our legs and lick my cock into him," Earl panted.

I jumped to obey him. God, but it was a beautiful sight: Earl's cock greasily sliding inside Johnny's ass-ring. I hunkered down between both their legs and licked on the disappearing meat. Johnny's clenching pucker was right in my face, and I watched Earl's monster fucktool spread him open.

I slobbered all over Earl's creambag, laving his dark butternuts in a bath of spit. That was all that was left to eat, for Earl's huge dick was now embedded completely inside of Johnny. Johnny was trembling and thrashing, tossing his hair from side to side on the bed like he had a telephone pole stuck up his chute. I sensed that Earl was jabbing at Johnny's trigger, pushing the yielding assflesh deeper.

"Now suck that cock, Johnny," Earl commanded, pulling me to the head of the bed.

I got Johnny's head between my spread and kneeling legs and guided it onto my throbbing meat. Johnny started licking his piss off the insides of my thighs with his long thick tongue fully distended. Then he expertly sucked me while Earl set up a quick, hard driving rhythm in his asshole.

Earl's broad chest was as smooth as velvet and I caressed his hairless pecs and twisted his dark chocolate nipples till they stood up on his gorgeous, planed body. His belly was flat and heaving as he worked his cock in and out of Johnny's rump. I felt all over his sweaty form and trailed my fingers through the tightly wound pubic hairs, growing like tiny grapevine tendrils on his groin.

And then Earl touched my face, and took my cheeks between his palms and drew my mouth onto his fully open lips. It was as though his tongue shot the length of my body, inflaming my throat like a lightning bolt which burst all the way to my groin. I trembled in his arms and he held me fast to him. His tongue was electrifying, completely filling my mouth. His ripe purple lips against mine were hot cushions between the pressure of our teeth crushed together. Earl mouth-fucked me ravenously even as he drove his cock more frenziedly into Johnny's hole, stabbing us with his dick and his tongue.

Earl's deep-dicking was rapidly driving Johnny over the edge. He humped and hunched his butt back onto Earl's plugging joystick like a pro bottom-man. It was hot as hell and I was ready to come again. Johnny gnawed greedily on my root and Earl went into the throes of a wild ejaculation. He rared back and left me gasping for air.

"Here it comes boy!" he shouted. "Take my load."

Johnny grunted piggishly around my root and gobbled more frantically.

"Ah shit! Jesus!" Earl gasped, throwing all his weight into his thrusting groin and unloading his seed up inside of Johnny. Then he planted his mouth on me again, and I choked down his awesome tongue, spearing my throat with the same intensity as his cock. It wouldn't have surprised me if his tongue had started coming.

That was all it took; thinking that, I began hosing off inside of Johnny's mouth, and I shuddered and trembled out a monstrous gusher of spunk. Johnny swallowed greedily and sucked me harder, faster. Earl finished flushing his nuts with a violent, jolting spasm.

We all collapsed in a heap on the bed. Earl hauled his dark firehose out of Johnny's well-fucked ass and squeezed out the last dewdrops of semen onto Johnny's rump. Johnny rolled onto his back, and I could see he'd added a fresh spit of cream to the messy mattress. The smell of shot-off cum and piss was as thick as a blanket in the tight, closed space.

"You've been up to your usual tricks, haven't you, Johnny?" Earl said.

Johnny was sheepishly looking at me, and I could see the sullen, stubborn bully inside him struggling to stay alive. He gave it up when Earl added, "Just admit you're gay, Johnny, and get on with it. Forget all that redneck foolishness. Same thing I told you back at the farm. The first time I fucked you, you loved it. Admit it."

"Yeah," was all that Johnny said.

But I mentioned at the beginning that I was bothered by something. That's because, after Earl left, Johnny told me he loved me.

"And I won't ever treat you mean again," he said.

"If you keep your word on that," I said as I kissed him deeply, "we're going to have a problem in our relationship."

TATTOOED TRADE

❖ ❖ ❖

Then he turned sideways to the mirror, his huge cock jutting out in all its splendor, as though he knew I was watching and wanted me to see its full length and hardness. That's when I first noticed the dreaded symbol.

Tattooed Trade

Back when we were still in college, my buddy, Danny, and I often used to hunt together. Not out in the woods with nature and all, but right here in the inner city where we both grew up. What we hunted was men—and sex.

I'd lost track of Danny ever since I dropped out after three semesters while he went on to graduate. His folks still live here, though, and they tell me he's teaching out west somewhere—they don't hear from him either. The Perkinses, Danny's mom and dad, remain pretty good friends of my parents.

I'd moved away from home after I met some guy who asked me to live with him over on the west side of town. That worked out for about a year and a half, but it was he who moved on and left me his small efficiency.

My folks still lived in the same apartment in the old neighborhood, which had become more Puerto Rican and black. I believe my mother and father and the Perkinses were about the only two white families left there. Danny and I didn't have a lot in common, except that we were both late kids in our parents' lives. He'd be in his middle thirties now, same as I am.

None of this has much to do with anything except by way of explaining how I came to be staying by myself in my parents' place while they visited a sick relative down in Georgia. I'd gotten a call from my mom asking me to watch their apartment while they were gone for a week or so. Being sort of old and retired, they'd gotten paranoid and a little fearful of the strangers on their block, though in all the time they'd lived there, they'd never been bothered at all.

"It's just your perception," I always told them.

I had a week off coming anyway and actually looked forward to just lying around, catching up on my reading. I packed some jeans and tee shirts in an overnight bag—since it was summer and hot as hell, I figured I wouldn't be needing much else. I arrived at their little flat on Saturday morning, and they left that afternoon.

I sat on the stoop as their old '68 Ford turned the corner and disappeared. Looking around my old neighborhood, I saw that it had deteriorated a lot. I put it down to age, absentee landlords, unemployment, never enough money for too many kids, the works.

Three young Puerto Rican youths swaggered by, and I tried not to stare at them. They were shirtless and had beautiful bodies, and it was an effort not to cruise them. The one nearest me was drop-dead-gorgeous: hair so black it was bluish, and pecs and abs and well-muscled arms as splendid as a classical statue's. His Levi's were well-worn and bulged at his crotch—in fact, they were so white at his basket, they appeared to have been bleached. A rough blue cross was etched into the pumped-up muscle of his left arm.

I remembered a rule of thumb that Danny and I had strictly adhered to: "If they've got a Playboy bunny anywhere—on their shirt or in their car, on an earring, an amulet, or a chain, anything at all with that damned symbol on it—steer clear. Like a cross to a vampire, they're nothing but trouble if you're gay." Later, after a serious close call and two black eyes, he extended the taboo to include prison tattoos.

Well, over the years, that admonition had proven fairly accurate. Ignoring it one time with an irresistible young hustler had cost me a VCR, my wallet, and an expensive gold chain. I vowed to keep my nose clean in this tough neighborhood.

I sat on the stoop until it was nearly dusk. No one of any interest passed by. I got bored. Walking up the two flights of stairs to the third floor gave me a new respect for my parents' stamina. I guess they'd gotten used to it after all these years, and it was probably good for them. My folks had never changed anything in their four small rooms since I was a kid. The only difference I could see was that my old room was now my father's study. The wallpaper was peeling a bit more, the upholstery a little more worn, and the Oriental rug had definitely seen better days.

The small confines smelled musty and sort of sour. I'd noticed it the last time I visited. And Mom always kept it too dark and closed in for my taste. I switched off the air conditioner, pulled open the heavy drapes—the same ones we'd had when I was a child—and opened the window to air the place out. I got sort of a warm feeling as I sat down in my father's chair.

And a hotter one as I glanced into the open window in the apartment house across the street. The blinds were up, the drapes wide open, and the sash window lifted to the top. A young man was exercising before a mirror which faced me. The windows in these old apartments are low, the sill beginning right off the floor and extending to near the ceiling. I had a perfect view of his entire trim torso, both from behind and from the front, which I could see reflected in the full-length mirror owing to its angle a little off to the right.

The youth was wearing only a pair of white briefs, and they were so tight I could see his supple ass dimpling as he squatted and stood, doing a vigorous set of deep knee bends. His skin was light brown, his hair coal-black, as were his eyes. His features attested to a mixed descent probably Spanish and African. At any rate, he was the most handsome young man I'd seen in years, even cuter than the boy who'd passed earlier.

I suddenly remembered that my father had kept a pair of binoculars stored in his closet. When I was a kid, he had used them to keep an eye on me while I played in the street. I raced into their bedroom, threw open the closet door, and my fingers scrabbled along the top shelf. Sure enough, they were still there.

I hurried back, perched on the edge of Dad's chair, and focused them on the athletic body of the boy. His rigorous calisthenics had bathed his lithe torso in a glistening sheen of sweat. I could see every bead as it trickled down his smooth, planed back. Though well-developed, he didn't appear to have overdone it. His skin was taut and toned like an exaggerated swimmer's build, a model for late-adolescent youth. He looked about nineteen. His underwear was wet with perspiration and, in the mirror, I could make out the folded length of his heavy dark cock and thick black pubes. I immediately threw a boner.

Twilight descended and it grew darker outside. "If only he'd turn on a light," I thought, straining my eyes to see. As if reading my thoughts, he disappeared from sight for a minute, and then a soft warm glow illuminated his room. He returned and stood before the mirror.

But he didn't continue exercising. Instead, he stood posing before his image, profiling and admiring the perfection of his body. He'd turn this way and that, pumping up his glorious muscles, caressing them, loving himself. I say the last because there was a definite swelling in his groin. I fine-tuned the binoculars on his reflection in the mirror and watched as his cock lengthened, straining toward the waistband of his briefs, then slipping out. His big uncut cock-knob was now throbbing just below his navel.

He pushed his shorts halfway down and clutched his meat in his fist. I threw the binoculars to the side table and skinned out of my jeans. I stood naked and watched in fascination as he started masturbating. My cock was hard as a fist and leaking lube juice all over my hand.

I felt a curious kind of intimacy with him as we jacked off together. Then he turned sideways to the mirror, his huge cock jutting out in all its splendor, as though he knew I was watching and wanted me to see its full length and hardness. That's when I first noticed the dreaded symbol.

There on his right arm muscle was a tattoo—a doubly bad omen, since it was a crudely drawn Playboy bunny. It was obviously amateurish, recognizable as one of those which prison inmates confer upon one another.

That didn't stop me from blowing my nuts when he shot off all over the mirror. The boy turned quickly, leaned back, and furiously pounded on his meat. Ropy streams of cum arched out and ran in silver strands down the surface of the mirror. He took a step forward and wiped his greasy cock through his own milk.

My knees buckled, and cum juice poured out of my working fist. I didn't bother to try and catch it, but let my semen spurt onto the rug, great globules of whitish milk pouring from between my wide-spread thighs.

His light went out just after that, and I dropped the drapes back into place. Since the next day was Sunday and I was used to sleeping late, I stayed up reading long after midnight.

In the morning while my coffee was brewing, I walked to the corner and bought the *Times*. I sat drinking and reading the paper on my stoop. The door across the way opened and closed, and he sat down on the steps opposite me. He was wearing only a pair of red shorts, with no shirt or shoes. He appeared to have just awakened, as he kept stretching and yawning. He tossed his head in a casual salutation as our eyes met. I returned it with an indifferent wave.

I generally kept the paper before my face, casting surreptitious glances in his direction whenever I'd turn a page. On one of those page-turnings, I noted that he'd spread his legs a little wider. The leg holes of his shorts gaped open, and I could see into the darkness of his groin. Staring down the empty street, he acted as if he were unaware of my presence.

But when I looked across at him again, he was still staring down the street, but had one hand up his shorts leg, obviously fondling his genitals. I just couldn't look away, and after a few moments of this, felt myself getting hard. Behind the paper, I palmed my cock.

He acted oblivious to my gaze as he drew out a full erection that stretched down his inner thigh. He started openly manipulating himself. I'd never witnessed such a brazen display as he openly caressed his stiff boner right there on the street. I dropped all pretense of reading and gawked wide-eyed at him.

He suddenly turned his head, and our eyes locked. My breathing became raspy and shallow. There was a challenge in his brooding gaze as he looked from me to his crotch, then back again. He licked his long, distended tongue fully around his full, fleshy lips, and there was no mistaking his intentions.

I threw all caution to the winds and walked across the street on trembling legs, my coffee and paper forgotten. When I was halfway toward him, he tucked his prick back inside his shorts, but the crimson head still protruded, leaving a slimy trail in the thick black hair on his leg. The nearer I drew to him, the more attracted I became. His upper torso was completely hairless, but oddly, his legs were as woolly as a bear's.

He stared at me defiantly, making no attempt to conceal his swollen cock, muscle-jerking the exposed glans so there was no way I could miss it.

I tried to act casual as I introduced myself. "I grew up over there," I lamely said, jerking my head at my parents' house.

"Oh yeah," he said, gruffly, surly. "So whatcha doin' back?" he half-sneered.

I explained my situation.

"My name's Raoul," he said as I concluded, shaking my hand with a well-calloused palm. "Looking for some action, man?"

I was nervous as hell, and he couldn't have missed my obvious trembling, not to mention my near-drooling attraction. All I needed was to get beaten up by a tough hustler right across the street from my parents' house—nevermind the danger of getting their house ripped off.

As a consequence, I turned him down: "Not today. I'm kinda busted." I tried to sound as butch as he did.

"C'mon, man, I know you want it," he said lasciviously, persistently. He pulled his cock out again. "You'd just love some of this Rican dick."

I cursed myself for ever crossing the street. I'd have to be here a week, and there was no telling what he and his friends could do to me in that time. "Look, man, let's just forget it. I don't want any trouble."

"Ain't gonna be no trouble if you'll come up to my room for a few minutes."

By continuing to stand there, I was getting in deeper all the time. My cock was already leaking pre-cum through my jeans. I made one last effort to extricate myself from this dilemma, "I don't have any money on me."

What he said next convinced me to follow him up the stairs: "Mirrors reflect everything, you know? I kinda liked what I saw last night."

His room was Spartan, to say the least—only a bare mattress on the floor, one chair and a milk carton next to it. There was another full-length mirror, this one mounted horizontally beside the make-shift bed. Raoul immediately stripped off his shorts and lay down on it.

I quickly followed suit, expecting this to be a quick blowjob that might cost me twenty bucks, but at least I'd get to jack off while servicing him. It started out that way, with him growling, "Suck me, man."

He was almost animal-like in his roughness, grabbing me by the head and propelling his cock down my throat without any preliminaries at all. He had a nice juicy prick, though, and I hungrily lip-stroked his thick, uncut shaft. His belly started heaving and he made piggish grunting sounds as I swallowed his dickmeat all the way to his furry ball-sac. His hairy nuts rolled in their bag when I squeezed on them. Meanwhile, I jerked myself off with my other hand.

It sort of angered me that he seemed so uninterested in reciprocating in any way, totally involved in his own satisfaction and not a thought in his head of gratifying me. He even kept his hands laced behind his head for the longest time. I did my best to stimulate him, licking and slobbering my way up and down his underside tube, laving his balls, cupping his nuts. His cock stayed hard, but all he wanted me to do was suck on him. Every time I'd stray from his dick, he'd push me back. As I watched myself in the mirror, I felt almost as detached as if I were looking at a porno flick.

In my anxiety to awaken some sort of response in him, or at least get a little stimulation myself, I once took his hand from the side of my head and guided it to my throbbing hard-on. He jerked it away as if he'd touched a snake.

I made ever more frenzied efforts to make him come, actually tiring a bit from working on pure trade. He just lay there like an unresponsive slab of meat—granted, it was prime, but I was bored nonetheless.

And then a perverse idea struck me. It hit me all at once, the complete equation: the tattoo; prison; probably went in early, with him young and good-looking; his fascination with himself; his now passive attitude; and, finally, that come-on remark he'd made about liking what he'd seen. I figured I was as strong as he was, and could easily defend myself if necessary.

I suddenly pulled off his cock and, before he could say a word, rolled him onto his stomach. I put my hands on his thin waist and pushed down hard with all my weight.

"Stay right there!" I barked in the harshest voice I could muster.

He looked surprised as he twisted his head and asked, "What the fuck are you doing?"

I didn't answer, but dived between his asscheeks and started tonguing up his hole. He had a bittersweet, funky taste that was somehow mellow. He clenched his ass-ring tightly and tried to tighten his buttcheeks. I dug into him feverishly. He started trembling and shivering. At last, a hint that he was human. Then, almost immediately, another hint—his pucker voluntarily relaxed. I swabbed his asswalls until he was positively gaping.

I straddled him and brought my swollen, dripping cockhead up to his now well-slobbered bunghole. His head thrashed from side to side and he started gasping, "No! No, please don't!" But his arms remained rigidly flung straight out, negating his loud protests. I drooled a long string of spit into my hand, greased up my cock, palmed his man-cleavage apart, and pressed my flared cock-knob inside him. "Oh God, no! Don't fuck me, man. Don't fuck me!" he panted. His ass was pushing back onto my dick, belying the message of his screams.

I sank one inch up his butt, and he quivered beneath me. I worked one more in, then more, then a little more. I held my cock rigidly still, muscle-jerking inside his guts. His fuck-chute relented and relaxed, drawing more of my prick into his warm guts. Raoul moaned and his breathing came in heavy gasps. He didn't take his eyes from the mirror.

"Oh shit! Oh fuck, you're fucking me!" he groaned.

He clenched his fists and dug them into the pillow. I ground relentlessly into him, and he pumped his loins to meet my thrusts. I reached around his flat, heaving belly and caught his root in my fist. His cock was even harder than before. Penile saliva leaked out and coated my hand as I stroked his thickly veined shaft. He hunched his hips into my hand and forced my cock deeper inside him.

Forcefully, I pulled him back into a dog fuck. Half-squatting with bent knees above him, I mauled his ass, plugging him with everything I had. He sighed contentedly when I squeezed and kneaded his tight nipples till they stood like tiny mountains on the plains of his pecs. I clapped both palms onto his asscheeks and pried them as wide apart as they would spread.

Alternately slapping each quivering mound with ever-increasing intensity, I snarled into his ear, "Take my fuck, you little punk! Get that goddamned cock up your ass."

"No! No! No!" he continued breathlessly. "Don't fuck me, *Papi*, don't fuck me!"

I shoved my cock all the way to his trigger. "Feel me! I want you to feel that dick your butt." I pounded on his trembling ass more vigorously than ever.

"*Oooh, sabroso*," was all he sighed. I could see in the mirror his face contorted with pleasure.

His buttocks were burned an angry red when I relented. "Tell me you like it, then! Say you like my cock in your ass. Tell me!"

"Oh God yes, Daddy!" he moaned. "*¡Me gusta!* I love your cock up my ass!"

"Show me then. Show Daddy how much you love getting fucked."

"I wanna ride you. I wanna fuck onto your dick."

A complete transformation had come over his face. He lay back onto me and twisted his body around, one leg passing over my chest until he sat astride me with his dripping root stretched over my belly, my cock still embedded deep inside him. He bucked like a demented colt as he rode my prick in and out of him. His eyes were slits and his teeth clenched, his lips twisting in an ecstatic grimace.

The sullen piece of trade I'd lain down with had finally awakened. Raoul had become a wild thing, pressing his whole body tightly against me and deep-tonguing inside my mouth. He never stopped hunching his hips as he milked off my root. We swapped slobber, and he nearly sucked my tongue out of my throat. Our images in the mirror beside us were forgotten. Raoul concentrated on working his ass muscles like a milking machine, slowly drawing me out, then crashing down while mumbling, *"¡Bueno, que bueno!"*He played with my balls and twisted my tits. He caressed my chest and shoulders. He started making love to me and love to himself.

He jacked himself in furious strokes, and I felt his ejaculation start when he ground down onto my pubic bone.

"I'm gonna come, man!" he needlessly yelled.

Already, spurts of jism were flying across my belly and chest.

Raoul had that milky kind of cream that shoots long, streaming jets an unbelievable distance. While my cum was blowing up his ass, his spewing milk splattered all over my face and into my hair. One glob hit the wall behind us. His cock-honey coated my whole body. He slumped across me and glued us with his cream, and just then, my own orgasm spasmed like a jolting aftershock—he looked pleased.

He slid off me and we lay side by side. He smiled and snagged a pack of cigarettes from the milk crate beside us. Lighting one for each of us, he leaned on one arm and looked at me.

"How did you know?" he asked, not alluding to what he meant.

"Just instinct, I suppose," I answered, then asked him if he needed any money.

"Nah. But I'd like to buy you a beer sometime—get to know you better."

As I caressed his smooth-muscled arm that bore the indelibly depicted Playboy bunny, I was reminded that all rules have exceptions.

RETURN OF THE SOLDIER

❖ ❖ ❖

Ling was a tight little bundle of joyful electricity, now unbound and flailing in my arms. I clutched his coltish, supple limbs, and he thrashed and trembled atop me. . .I gasped and panted in anguish as he forced my cock down his slender throat. . .

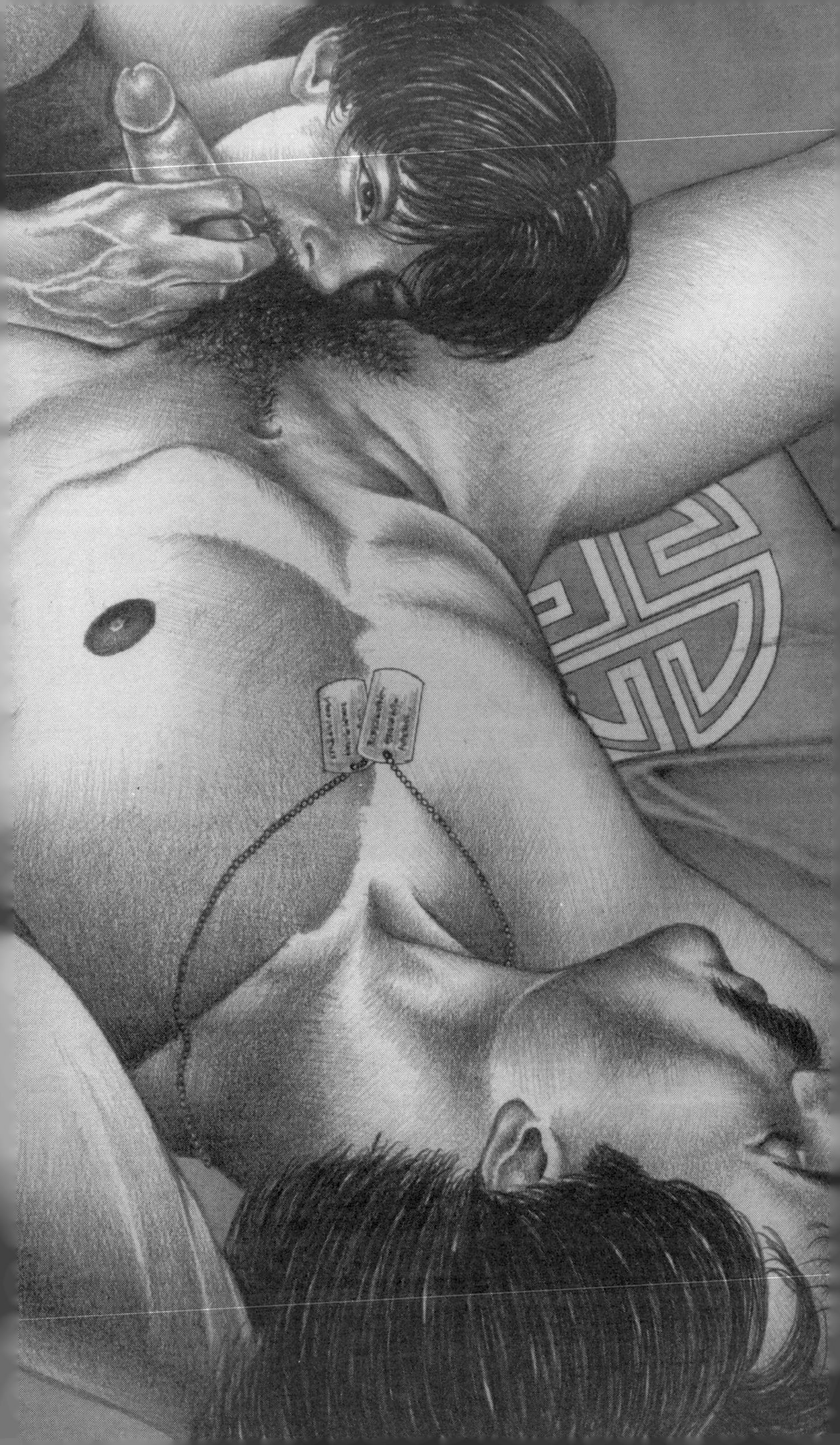

Return of the Soldier

It wasn't easy going back to Vietnam after such a long time had elapsed. I still had a lot of bad memories from the time of the war. I'd been nineteen then and had had a love affair with another GI, a guy who never made it back to the states. I guess half the reason I returned was to remember him. I even dug out my old dog tags and hung them round my neck again, shivering at the memories brought back by that gesture.

I had just turned forty, and it seemed important to me at the time. I'd managed to keep my same weight and stay pretty much in shape by working out at the local Y. Though my hair is salt and pepper now, I've been told I'm still pretty hunky. At least one boy thought so.

The first time I saw Ling Sanh, he was furiously pedaling his bicycle down the overcrowded streets of Saigon, his lithe, muscular legs pumping away at the pedals, the afternoon sun bronzing his trim, bare back with glistening sweat.

I was sitting in a small park on a bench in the rebuilt center of the battle-scarred city, idly absorbing all the changes since the war. I first noticed the boy as he flew past my resting place. Besides his tennis shoes, he was wearing only tight, red shorts that clung to his cute Asian ass-globes as he stood off the seat. The butt-hugging shorts cleaved his firm, rounded cheeks as if they had been sprayed there like a second skin. He seemed to be about the same age as I had been when I was a soldier in the war.

The boy glanced over in my direction as he passed. I shot him a friendly smile and was rewarded when he returned it. He disappeared down the street. I sat there about another ten minutes, watching joggers and cyclists pass on the winding road in the park. I caught my breath when I noticed the boy returning, on foot this time.

I spotted him coming around the bend of the jogging path, idly tossing a tennis ball in the air as he walked, catching it accurately behind his back each time. As he neared my bench, he threw the ball higher and higher, demonstrating his agility and youthful grace. His trim body was angular and compact, and his face had that finely chiseled, preternatural beauty which is often obtained when the inheritances of all the human races are combined. There was a subtle interplay between Asian and African in his delicate features.

The boy's warm brown eyes met mine, and I began to feel my pulse in my groin. His engaging smile was matched and duplicated in his impishly slanted eyes, eyes that flashed with a dark lustre like agate marbles.

I couldn't stop staring at his flat belly, his hairless chest with rosy nipples, and the small bulge at his youthful crotch. The sinewy muscles of his thighs were striated in wave-like planes, bunched and taut, as were his well-developed calves. He paused and dawdled in front of me, bouncing the tennis ball back and forth between his hands. Then he missed it, and the fumble looked deliberate. He chased the ball into a grassy area, and I grew delirious with lust as he bent over to retrieve it and I saw his pert little bubblebutt seemingly about to burst the seam of his shorts.

My breathing grew shallow as the boy sprawled on the lush green grass right opposite me. He lay back lazily and turned his body a few times as though seeking a comfortable position. He opened his legs, V'd straight in my direction. He palmed languidly over his groin, and I detected a definite swelling at the juncture of his well-formed thighs.

I clutched my big fucktool as it began snaking down my leg and kneaded the shank inside my jeans. I tried to conceal its stretching length from passersby. That became an impossible task as Ling Sanh lolled his youthful, black-haired head on the grass, turning sideways to face me. His hair was lustrous with bluish tints, and as straight as if it had been ironed. It fell forward, partially concealing one fervent eye that carried a look of lasciviousness from under his thin, arched brows. His smile was tantalizing and alluring, sensuous and hinting at sexual delights.

I felt awkward as hell, having no experience with picking up Asian hustlers, since that is what I figured him for. A man of my age gets used to their seductive ways in the states, so I figured that *look* was universal. In any case, the kid had gotten me so hot with his salacious display, wild horses couldn't have prevented me from approaching him. I was painfully conscious of the lube-juice that drooled out of the cock-knob pressing against my thigh as I rose and walked toward him.

"What's your name?"

"Ling Sanh," said the youth around a crooked grin that spread almost from ear to ear. His next words made me almost delirious with lust. "You like make boy-fuck?"

"I like you," I stammered, my heart beating so loudly, I knew he must hear it.

"You are American, no?" Ling Sanh asked with a cock of his head.

I nodded.

"Like my father. See." Here he pulled a small plastic case from the waistband of his shorts, opened it to reveal a well-worn photo of an American GI. The man was an incredibly handsome, light-skinned black man, himself probably of mixed blood. That combination of various races, in the person of Ling, had produced one of the most ravishing boys I'd ever encountered.

"How much money?" I nervously asked.

Ling Sanh shrugged his slight shoulders, opened his almond eyes very wide. "A present, maybe," he said with a mischievous grin.

The top of his head, crowned with his dark black hair, came only to my shoulders as he stood beside me. I was trembling with anxiety, so nervous that my legs shook a trifle. We talked a little about the war on our short stroll to my hotel. He only knew of it from his history classes.

Once in my room, Ling Sanh wasted no time, but stripped from his shorts and tennis shoes straightaway. There was a bold and endearing gleam in his eyes as he sprawled across my bed. I could only stare in wonder at his coppery torso, his young penis already hard as he masturbated himself in slow, wistful strokes. Though of an average size, his pinkish, slender shaft jutted at an angle from a dark patch of coal black pubic hair, wiry and soft looking, like ebony down. He was uncircumcised, and his foreskin was stretched tightly around the middle of his glans.

I peeled out of my clothes before his lustful gaze. His smallish features gleamed with boyish delight as my cock slid from the waistband of my Jockeys and saluted my navel. I pushed them down, kicked them off, and fell beside him, my entire body aquiver with anticipation.

Ling opened his young, molasses-colored arms and snuggled into my embrace. I kissed his soft tender lips, and his slender tongue darted into my mouth like an excited fish in a feeding frenzy. I felt his pulsing cock pressing into my groin as he ground his trim flanks against me, framing my groin with his smallish pelvis. Pre-cum seeped from my engorged cockhead and slimed our loins as we thrust against one another.

The boy's dark skin was unbelievably smooth as I caressed every tufted hollow and moist crevice of his youth. He trembled in my enfolding arms as I dug my palm up his crack, feeling the dampness between his youthful cheeks. Lovingly, tenderly, Ling forced me to my back. He straddled my thumping belly and I felt the heat of his pucker as he glided his lithe buttocks up and down my cock, propelling my dick hard onto the base of his spine, and softly moaning.

Ling was a tight little bundle of joyful electricity, now unbound and flailing in my arms. I clutched his coltish, supple limbs, and he thrashed and trembled atop me. I half-twisted his lithe body and gnawed at his silken armpits, licked the soft downy hair in his sweet-smelling hollow, and tasted his spunky sweat. His delicate hands wandered through the thicket of fur on my chest, catching my tightened nipples and pinching them harder in delight. He laved a slurping trail to my crotch and held my rigid cock aloft.

Ling distended his tongue to its fullest and gave little dick-licking flicks to my circumcised crown. Squeezing my heavy shaft at the base, he washed my leaking knob. Then he dragged my fat urethral tube through his delicate lips. I gasped and panted in anguish as he forced my cock down his slender throat until I could see the cockhead bulging in his neck.

I dragged him off my fucker and pulled him back onto me. He kept trying to strain from my grasp and get back onto my root.

"No! No!" I panted. "You're gonna make me come too soon."

"I will make you come two times," he said with a wicked grin.

I wanted to fuck this boy more than any other in my life. But I reluctantly gave in to his pleading.

"Let me suck it, let me suck it."

I guided his slender torso around till his delectable ass was in my face. I sighed deeply as I once more felt his hot mouth engulf my cock and eagerly begin to feed on me.

I palmed his buttcheeks apart and tongued my way up his ass-trench. I licked and swirled my tongue all over his tight little asshole, and slurped noisily at his bittersweet funk. He groaned around my embedded joint and clenched his hole, flexed and dimpled his perfect ass. I ate into his sweet young rectum like a starving man, slobbering and greasing up his clenching hole. A delicious nectar of hot sexflesh filled my nostrils and danced a wild tango on my taste buds as I hungrily reamed Ling's little Asian pucker.

The taste of his delectable ass drove me over the edge. My entire midsection trembled and quaked as the first jolting spasms of ejaculation crested, held taut and tense, then broke over into a spilling, tumbling wave of divine release.

"I'm gonna shoot!" I needlessly wailed around Ling's butt. His feverish lips increased their tempo and he moaned an encouraging snarl. "I'm coming, boy! Take it, take it!"

He gasped and sucked harder. Then he reached down and squeezed my balls firmly, and the juice hit my cum-tube at high speed. I arched my hips and let him devour my spurting seed. The kid gobbled crazily on my gushing organ.

"Oh, God!" I screamed as the near-torturous paroxysms struck between my legs. "Take it, boy! Take my milk!"

Ling began clenching and grinding his loins, his cock burrowing between my pectorals and sawing hard against the friction of my slickened skin. I felt him spurting cum like a yearling, spasming little bursts as he rutted on my body. His spitting seed was hot between our pressed flesh, his belly and my chest. His asshole in my face gaped open as he shot and I tongue-fucked him till his shuddering ceased.

The violence of my shattering orgasm stilled to a deep and satisfying warmth. Ling pulled off my dripping cock and threw himself back around till he was once more facing me. I lay by his side with his head cradled in the nape of my neck, savoring the beauty of his youth. I held his shivering torso against me, and a flush of buried emotions overcame me.

Feeling half-asleep, and sex-drugged, I flashed random pictures from the past across the scrims of my half-closed eyes. This boy—thousands of them. Us and Them, what we'd done, what had happened, the way it was. The way it was—they'd whipped our ass! And for some very strange reason, that was not an unsatisfying thought.

We lay there in the warm afterglow of our spent coupling, holding and stroking one another. This was the way it should have been. Always. Ling told me that his mother had been a prostitute during the war, but had fallen in love with his father. He was another guy who never made it home.

"But that was then," he said as he straddled my loins again. "Now you make me come again."

Under his stroking fingers and thousand kisses on every patch of my body, my erection strained upward once more. Ling Sanh clutched my slab of hard dick-meat in his fist and held it rigidly upright. He squatted his haunches above my pole and gently lowered his buttocks till the flaring head of my cock was pressing against the tender flesh of his sex-pocket. With a deft agility, he eased the crown inside his ass-ring. I watched with fascination as my cock disappeared up his warm, velvet vise.

Clenching his teeth, and with a painful grimace on his face, Ling worked my meat up his chute. Ling started jacking on his cock and moaning and sighing heavily as he struggled to get my log up his channel. I tweaked and twisted at his hard tight nipples, caressed his flanks, and squeezed his flat belly from both sides, so small my hands could clutch him front and back. Then when he was fully impaled, he lay atop me, kissing and swaying his lower back, undulating his narrow hips and fucking himself on my cock. I felt the heat of his soft insides, the pressure of my knob against his trigger, the melting warmth of his assflesh.

I began to arch my spine, pressing up and deeper into him. He was everything I'd known he would be, and more. He groaned and reared back from our kiss, tossed his head from side to side as I rode into his depths, his straight black hair flailing against my cheeks and shoulder. Ecstasy was in his burning eyes and on his sweet young face.

I clutched his cock and started jacking him off in time with his thrusting loins. I stroked the satiny skin of his ass with my other hand as he bucked madly atop my pounding flanks. His swollen penis flared and his cockhead emerged near crimson from the folds of angry foreskin that I peeled back, unhooding his gorgeous dark prick, still leaking semen from his last climax.

Our thrashing bodies were soon bathed in sweat as I undulated my fuck into him. I remembered his words from the park: "You like boy-fuck?" Ling was the essence of that compound word; his perfect butt, made for fucking, a boy-fuck with a fuck-boy unlike any I'd ever experienced.

Inside of Ling's ass, it felt like a furnace of licking flames, leaping and dancing through my groin as Ling drilled himself repeatedly up and down my burning cock. He increased the tempo of his fiery fuck, driving both of us to the limits of endurance.

Then he began wildly fucking himself on my cock, gasping and gibbering in his language as he milked me with his ass-muscles, rippling sparks of glory up and down my embedded root. I pushed his little hips all the way down on my grinding crotch, and he gyrated his pelvis and screwed himself all the way to my balls.

Skimming my hands all over his tight body, I ground my flanks up and down, matching his masturbation, stroke for stroke. He bucked on my dick and thrashed madly about, taking my fuck faster and faster.

I opened my legs as wide as a frog's and pulled his squirming ass harder onto my groin. Sitting up, I clutched him about the waist and we hunched our fuck while madly kissing, Ling's legs wrapped completely around me, feet crossed and locking us together. His cock pressed hard between our bellies, rutting into the friction of our ever more fevered exertions.

I grabbed his cock and jacked it between us.

"I come! I come!" he wailed.

I pounded my hips harder and faster against him. I took his little ass and savagely pushed and pulled it on and off my cock. I felt his cum pumping out of his cock and I jacked him more forcefully. Jets of creamy cum blew off between us and lathered up our sweating bodies.

I went off in his ass like a hydrant. Mauling his mouth and holding him as tightly to me as possible, I unloaded my milk in shuddering blasts. His eruption ended with a jerking spit of seed that splattered hot on our grinding skin.

I stroked his heated and quivering form, and he melted in my arms. I felt the last drops of jizz draining into him and his head collapsed on my shoulder. I fell back with him in a tight embrace and we held one another till our spasms had subsided. He lay still for so long, I thought he'd fallen asleep on my chest. His breathing had grown even, and it quite possibly was the most delicious moment I was to spend with him.

My wilting cock slipped from his hole, and he adjusted his form so that his body was lying aslant mine, his damp groin on my thigh, his leg drawn over mine and his face resting at my neck.

"It is good?" he whispered into my ear.

"It is wonderful, Ling. Perfect," I said softly.

"I can stay with you?" he asked.

"Forever, I wish," I whispered. I felt so good, I wanted to weep. It was the first time I truly understood the expression "cry with happiness." "Forever."

But forever only happens in fantasy. I did keep him with me the rest of the time that I was there. I can honestly say I have never known a boy of such radiant beauty, his body and his spirit, boy of the rainbow. I never really figured out if Ling was a hustler or not. I didn't ask him for fear of being told. He never asked for anything, but I gave him money every day, and we shared all our meals in restaurants.

On the last day I was there, I bought Ling a shiny red motorcycle. He was sitting astride it as my plane taxied down the runway. It seemed that my bitter memories were salved as the plane angled up and Vietnam fell away below me. Now when I remember that sad, lovely country, I recall the beauty and grace of my time with Ling Sanh.

HONEYSUCKLE

❖ ❖ ❖

*He held me
by my ass with one hand
and caressed my naked torso
with the other. No amount
of fantasizing and
jacking off had quite prepared
me for my first real man.
I went wild...*

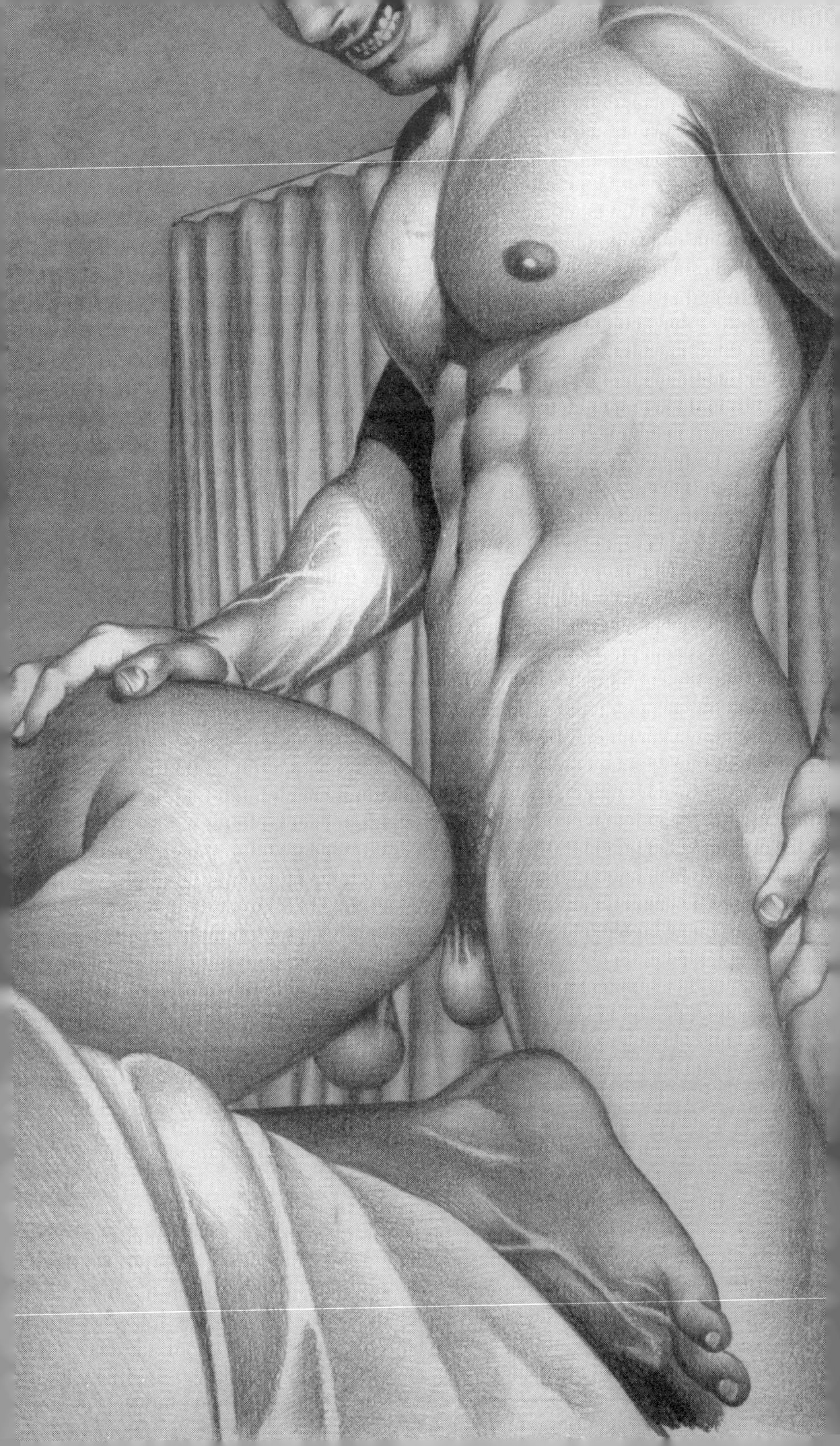

Honeysuckle

I doubt that anyone from the rural community in Alabama where I grew up would recognize me these days. I'm not the same skinny little black kid my folks put on the Greyhound bus bound for Chicago, back in the early Sixties.

I had just turned eighteen and there was no work at all back home. Dad's sister had moved up there several years earlier, and she assured me I could find a job in the factory where she worked. I had never even left the state before, so it was with a real spirit of adventure that I set off. My education began almost as soon as the bus pulled out of the station.

It was dusk and I was sitting in an aisle seat next to an older, white gentleman who dozed off as soon as we hit the highway. The bus was full. The two seats directly across from me were occupied by two old ladies, both reading books. I slouched down in the seat and stretched my legs out in front of me. Then I caught the profile of a young white guy who was in front of the old ladies, one row up from me and across the aisle. He looked to be in his middle twenties, with red hair and freckles.

He had turned half-sideways and was studying my highly polished shoes. Then his gaze crawled up my legs to my face, and he smiled. I smiled back. His eyes were near the color of a bluebottle fly, almost iridescent. Being a friendly sort of guy, but not having much experience with strange white men since we rarely saw any in the all-black area of my home, I nodded my head. He did the same and winked at me.

I naively winked back at him, not understanding a thing about the meaning of attention from a man. His face lit up like he'd just run into an old friend, and his smile revealed a large gap between his two front teeth, giving him a look of boyish innocence. Then his eyes unlocked from mine and started raking back down my lean body. I had the first little inkling that something wasn't quite right when he deliberately stared long and hard at my crotch.

I come from a very religious family, five brothers and sisters, all quite close. I'm the oldest, and though I knew all about the sex thing, I'd never really had a girl. My parents were strict and had kept all of us kids on the straight and narrow. I was wearing my very best Sunday-go-to-meeting clothes, as all my family called our dark blue suits. I had a fresh haircut and felt pretty good about myself. But the way the guy kept looking at me, I thought perhaps there was something wrong with my pants. I checked to make sure I was zippered up and that my dick hadn't crawled out or something. I could feel my cock suddenly starting to swell between my legs, and the man's stare was like a burning flame, making me hot down there.

Mama had splurged at the five-and-dime and bought me new underwear for my trip, and right then, I was glad I'd asked for the Jockey kind rather than the boxers I usually wore. I was boning up, big time, and at least the tight briefs kept me from poking out a country mile. But the pouch of my underwear was getting tight, and there was no way the red-haired man could miss the definite swelling as my teenage sap started running high.

So when his gaze finally returned to my face, I had an embarrassed look plastered across my smallish features. I scrunched back down in my seat and stared across the sleeping man and out the window. It was starting to get dark and the bus was dimly lit, the nearest illumination coming from above the two reading ladies. I sneaked a look back to the front and the guy had thankfully turned around. All I could see of him was his elbow, protruding into the aisle. I couldn't see who was in the seat beside him, but I heard snoring coming from that direction, so I assumed the person must be asleep.

That was confirmed when the friendly guy's elbow started moving. I knew what jacking off looked like when I saw it; I did it myself a couple of times a day to keep the blue balls away. "He couldn't really be jacking off right here on the bus," I thought. And he wasn't, really; he was just acting like he was. I knew, because he got up from his seat and stood in the aisle a minute before walking past me to the bathroom at the rear of the bus. He made sure I saw his hard-on as he passed.

He grinned down at me with the most wicked leer I'd ever beheld, like we were sharing a secret or something. My cock got as hard as a poker and I looked around, but no one was paying any attention to me. After a few minutes, the redhead returned and stopped in the aisle beside me. He leaned over real close to my ear, and whispered.

"Want something to help you with that?" he asked, nodding toward my groin.

I didn't have any idea what he was talking about, except that it related to my dick. But I nervously nodded. Then his hand came from behind him, and he slipped something into my jacket pocket, smiled once more and sat down again. My hand shook a little as I nervously reached into the pocket. He'd dropped a rubber in there. Wet. Full of cum.

While my hand was still in there, feeling it all gooey and slickened up with lube, he turned around in the seat again. When he saw that I wasn't going to beat the shit out of him or something, he motioned with a jerk of his head toward the bathroom. I may have been a dumb kid from the country, but I didn't need any instructions on what to do with the rubber.

Slipping from my seat, I made my way to the rear of the bus and entered the tiny cubicle. I dropped my pants and underwear all the way to my ankles and leaned back on the little metal sink. I held my dress shirt up with my chin and clutched my hard cock at the fat base. The guy had shot a good, heavy load of cum into the rubber and it slid on real easy, gliding over my uncut knob and skinning back the dick-flesh till it was purple and pebbled all over with tiny nubs that were ultra-sensitive to touch.

I'd never done anything like that before, jacked off in another man's rubber. His juice was still warm and gummy, becoming frothy and white against my dark cock as I furiously beat my meat. Thinking about the guy's dick having been there where mine was, thinking about him shooting his wad into the same thing I was fixing to fill, well, it was enough to make me blow my nuts almost straight away.

I punched out my hips, grabbed my balls, and dragged the bag down low while I fisted that fucker as hard as I could. Damn, but it felt good. My legs started trembling and my nuts drew up in their sac. I felt a real gusher of jizz start pumping out.

Usually when I come, it bursts out of my cock in long ropy streams, shooting over my head if I'm lying down and haven't gotten off that day. But this time, I was able to concentrate on my spunk as it flowed out into the rubber and mixed with the redhead's juice. Talk about milk gravy! The end of that rubber bloated out and swelled up like a mushroom as I milked off my load.

Shaking all over like one of my daddy's old hounds when it was fucking a bitch, I squeezed off the last of my seed and drained it into the rubber. Then I pulled it off and tossed it into the trash, wiped off my dick with a paper towel, and redressed. The bus was almost completely dark when I returned to my seat. The redhead turned around with a cool, knowing look on his face, and we shared another grin. I kind of liked the guy and liked what had happened. Something about sharing a secret with that stranger made me feel good.

I fell asleep while the bus roared on through the night. Dawn was just breaking when I woke up. I had a piss-hard that wouldn't wait. The bus was just swerving around a corner and into another station, I didn't know where. Fortunately, it was a pretty big town and the driver announced we'd be stopping here for breakfast. The redhead was about three people in front of me as we filed out the door. I made a beeline for the rest room and saw him doing the same.

Another bus had arrived just before ours, and the place was full as I pushed through the swinging doors. I didn't see my friend at the long row of urinals where guys were pissing, but I did notice an empty stall and made for that.

I'd never even heard of a glory hole, much less seen one. This one had to be a good six inches across, and well-used, by the look of the worn smooth edges. I hauled out my cock and stood above the bowl, flushing out a real morning, horsecock piss. I became aware of an eye at the hole watching me. There was no mistaking the redhead's face. I got a hard-on the instant I recognized him.

Then he leaned back on the stool and, without having to bend at all, I could see he had his cock in his fist and was pumping away on the fucker. His dick was long and almost as bright red as his pubic bush. Instinct took over from there. I quickly hung my suit jacket on the hook behind the door, dropped my drawers and sat down. My cock had never felt harder. We looked through the hole at the same time and watched each other masturbating. It was all I could do to keep from coming. Lube was running out of my dick like a dribbling faucet, and I had to hold my cock real tight at the base and not jack it for several minutes or I'd blow off.

Presently, the sounds of other men dwindled away and the bathroom grew so quiet, you could hear us breathing. Then the guy motioned for me to stick my cock through the hole. My legs trembled as I stood up. And then, it was like I'd waited all my life for the feel of that man's mouth as he started sucking my cock. I pushed my hips against the partition, reached to the top, and hung on for dear life as he engulfed my rod all the way.

Panting and gasping, he mouthed me up and down the underside of the tube, holding my cock at the base and slobbering all over the head, licking my uncut crown and swirling his tongue inside the foreskin. Then he sucked the fucker in all the way again and held my meat deep down his throat, milking me off with his rippling gullet muscles.

I lifted my feet from the floor and jabbed my cock in and out with smart little hunches of my hips. A glorious sensation of being sucked dry overcame me and I started shooting off. He began making little squealing noises of delight as he sucked my jizz into his mouth. I could feel he wasn't swallowing, but holding my dickhead just inside his lips and letting my cream fill his mouth. Shaking and trembling all over, I drained out the last of my juice. Then I plopped back exhausted on the toilet. He looked in at me and winked. His lips were compressed and he didn't say anything.

Then he leaned back on the stool again and got his cock in his hand. I put my eye to the hole to watch him jack off. The man had opened the front of his shirt and his red hair furred his chest all the way over his flat belly to the dense mass at his crotch. Then he looked at me with solemn eyes, and I watched in amazement as he started spitting my cum onto his dick.

Between that broad gap in his teeth, he was spraying out cum like a second shot, a long stream that he aimed straight for his root and splattered all over his cock and balls. We used to have spitting contests when I was a kid, and the one who could spit through his teeth always shot the longest. And old Red had that technique down perfect. He blew his nuts as my cum arched and streamed onto his dick. His sauce boiled out, and between our two loads, his whole crotch was soon soaked with jism. The smell of shot-off cum was so thick, I could practically taste it.

Red bought me a big country breakfast and he had a Danish and coffee. He said everybody called him Red, which I'd already figured, and I told him my name was Phillip. "Let's sit together the rest of the trip," he suggested. I jumped at the offer. We were lucky to get the two seats at the very back of the bus. I learned more that first full day on the road than in all the years of growing up.

"You taste like honeysuckle," Red whispered that night, as the bus was passing through Ohio. "Like when I was a kid, we'd suck the honeysuckle flowers and the juice was sweet and mellow. Can I call you that, my little Honeysuckle?" That's how I got my nickname and that's what he called me after he'd blown me again during the night.

My sister was waiting for me at the bus stop and I left with her, after Red gave me his address and asked me to visit him the following night. I wasn't quite prepared for the size of Chicago, and Laura laughed at my gawking as she drove me to her apartment. She and her husband had a spare room and I settled right in. I couldn't decide what thrilled me the most: my new life in the big city or my sexual coming of age. Let's just say that my dick stayed hard a lot.

"You be careful now, Phillip," Laura warned me as I took off the next night. "You don't know what this city can be like."

I sure didn't, but I knew that, as I rode the subway Red had told me to take, I was cruised at least three times. Maybe it had something to do with the tight white dress pants I'd chosen to wear, the ones from my senior prom. I located Red's apartment easily enough, a modest one-bedroom place on the third floor. Red was wearing a ratty old bathrobe when he answered the door, and I had some second thoughts about visiting him. But he practically dragged me in and asked me to sit on the couch. Then he took a seat opposite me in a wing chair.

"So," he said, moving his hands together in a worrying way as he fretted with his fingers, "you get settled in and all? You like the city?"

I allowed as to how I hadn't seen much of it, but liked what I had seen. "It sure is big," I said.

"Just like you," he said, smiling mischievously. "You and I are gonna make quite a team." I expected he'd start to come on to me then, but he sat back and acted as though he was waiting for something. I was a little fidgety myself, this being such a new experience for me, and Red offered me a beer.

"Thanks," I said as he handed it to me without touching me.

He sat back in his chair again and stared at me. I squirmed and got an erection. He could see it plainly beneath the thin white fabric, and he licked his lips, his eyes jumping between my face and my crotch. Again, I was glad for my new underwear.

I didn't know what the hell was going on, why we were just sitting there. He'd certainly known what I came there for, and I was horny as hell waiting for him to make his move. I didn't want to come right out and ask him to blow my dick or anything so crude as that, but I did keep my eyes glued to his groin. Red started tenting up, his robe gaping over his dick. The opening grew larger until the fat head came snaking out and he tried to push it down with no success. He looked irritated. The robe draped his legs and covered most of his chest, but fell away from that stunning hunk of cockflesh protruding from his groin. I couldn't help it, I licked my lips.

"Oh shit!" he exclaimed, like he was aggravated with me about something. "Let's fuck, Honeysuckle."

"About damn time," I thought, but I didn't say it.

He let the robe fall away, and I stood and undressed in front of him. Naked and hard, he started kissing on me. He started deep-tonguing into my mouth, his mouth-meat feeling like a cock down my throat. I swallowed and sucked on it like a starving man. I felt his pumped-up cock digging into my skinny belly, felt him lubing on me. I ground my hips against his hardness. He was rubbing those big palms of his all over my smooth, young back and driving me into a frenzy of lust. I felt near to coming just eating on his tongue that way.

He kneaded and squeezed on my asscheeks, gliding his palm sideways through my crack and teasing my hole with his finger. I wilted onto him and he grabbed me right off the ground. I wrapped my legs around his waist and my arms around his neck. He held me by my ass with one hand and caressed my naked torso with the other. No amount of fantasizing and jacking off had quite prepared me for my first real man.

I went wild in Red's bearhug. I would never have thought

anything could be so deliriously wonderful. Until. Until I felt him maneuvering his cock-knob up to my hole.

"Easy, baby. Easy," he said right into my mouth. "Slide down on it."

"Oh, God!" I moaned. Both his meaty hands were spreading my rump apart, his uncut head nudging up to my pucker. His dick slid just inside my ass-ring and I shivered in his arms. "Oh! Oh shit!" I grunted, feeling him pressing relentlessly into me.

"C'mon, c'mon, baby, you can take it," Red gasped.

He was pulling my ass harder onto his root, and the realization that I was getting fucked for the first time in my life nearly made me come. My dick was running snot between our pressed flesh, and I thought I would die on this man's cock. The pain was intense. He held me tighter than ever till my ass-ring relaxed. Suddenly, my body seemed to open, to receive him. I felt myself being filled with his root. The spasms of pain were replaced with a washing numbness which quickly became the most intense pleasure I'd ever experienced.

"Ah, man!" I sighed. "Fuck it in me. Fuck me!"

"Sweet ass, man. Sweet, young ass," Red grunted, working more meat up my chute. "Take all of me, Honeysuckle. Take my fuck!"

By now, he could've turned me loose and I would still be riding his cock. But he held me tightly to his hairy body and started pumping his hips, fucking up into my body with a raging passion. I got most of his thick red hair in both fists and held on for dear life as his fuck got even wilder. I clung to him and sucked on his tongue.

He got in me all the way and started jabbing at my trigger with his cockhead. Fully sheathed up to my guts, he held his cock fast against my prostate and muscle-jerked it so I could feel it throughout my entire body. It was like I was an extension of his cock, impaled forever and another vital organ of this handsome, hairy stud.

Waves of torturous ecstasy washed over me as Red fucked me full out. Standing up. Holding me tight onto him. Fucking into my virgin butt with a demented fury. Effortlessly, he held my slight torso to him and ground his penetration deeper than he'd been all along. Now I could feel the hairs on his cock with my sensitive assflesh. I could feel my teenage sap frothing in my half-crushed balls.

Red jackknifed his spine backward and held me a little off from him. "I'm fixin' ta come!" he panted. "Get it, baby! Take my load!"

By just grinding my cock against his hard hairy belly, I felt my own cum racing up the tube. "Come, man! Come in me!" I gasped.

"Oh shit!" he yelped.

I felt his cum filling me, fulfilling me. A shattering ejaculation bolted through my entire midsection and washed his belly in a bath of juice. His spunk kept shooting in my ass. My cum barreled out in swift racing streams, and Red fervidly watched me getting my nut all over his red-haired body.

Red sighed. "Ah yeah! Come, baby. Come!"

"Fuck me!" I screamed a final time, riding the hot waves.

"Jesus, man!" he growled. "What a fuck! What an ass!"

My discharged cock-honey rode on top of his pelt in thick, white globs. I couldn't remember shooting so much cum. Red's whole body was heaving, like I was riding on an animal in the throes of a fit.

We both panted and gasped for air. Red eased down to his knees with his dick still planted in my hole. My trembling legs hit the concrete floor and he had to hold me up as he slid his fat cock out of my well-fucked ass.

Suddenly, someone knocked at the door. Red cursed, snatching on his robe and racing for it. He mumbled low, but I thought I heard him say, "Another time." He kissed me good-night and I left, after promising I'd return two nights hence.

That time, the same scene. I went to Red's apartment, he kept me sitting there till he got so aroused, he took me to the bedroom and fucked the bejesus out of me. Then someone came to the door, and he told them he'd see them later. The third time, the same thing.

Now you've probably figured out what was going on a long time ago, but I was new at all this and it wasn't until about the fifth or sixth time that I figured out his scene. We'd just had a particularly athletic romp between the sheets, when some man barged in. Red had been so hot to get in my ass that he'd forgotten to lock the door.

The intruder stood over the bed and shook his fist at Red. "What the hell kinda pimp are you?" he shouted. "Keeping your new 'Honeysuckle' all to yourself!" But then he calmed down and we had a great threeway. Red apologized for not turning me out as he'd planned, and asked me if I was interested in being one of his boys.

"Don't think so, old buddy," I told him. "But thanks for the compliment." I toyed with the idea of being an independent, but Chicago is a big city. I never got around to charging anybody, so busy was I at giving it away.

Rich People

❖ ❖ ❖

Charlie yanked off my jacket and shirt. He practically tore my pants in half as he grappled me out of them. I pulled down his shorts to just his underwear. And then the kid got playful.

Rich People

"Spoiled brat, if you ask me," my friend, Carl, said. "Joey, he'll probably ask you to shine his shoes for him while you're toting his bags."

We were discussing the appearance in the hotel lobby of a particularly handsome young man who was checking in with an older couple, no doubt his parents. We'd been told they were VIPs, a multimillionaire newspaper publisher and his high society wife. They were at the registration counter of the magnificent Fairmont Hotel where Carl and I work as bellmen. The captain had signaled that it was my turn for the next party, and they were next.

The Fairmont is one of the last, grand old hotels of that period when the robber barons were making millions in the industrial revolution, and oil money flowed steadily into the hands of the Rockefellers, DuPonts, Astors, Lowells, and Cabots, captains of industry accumulating their initial wealth. All those people had stayed here in the past. Presidents and kings had enjoyed the Fairmont's marble floors, Oriental carpets, crystal chandeliers, heavy velvet drapes, brass so brightly polished it was hard to look at, antique furnishings, potted palms, and old wood paneling which gleamed as bright as that dawning age. You get the idea: class. And we still catered to that crowd.

"You just don't like rich people, Carl," I said. "You're at the wrong hotel."

"I just don't like rich *white* people," Carl answered. "If one of us makes it, fine by me. Like you."

Carl and I had had this discussion often in the past, after we both discovered we were gay. We're products of New Orleans' only slightly updated version of class distinction. Being black, you still see a lot of lines drawn in the racial sands. And Carl personally drew the line at fucking white boys.

I certainly understood Carl's attitude. He'd been on this job for eleven years, and would probably stay an equal number more, being treated pretty much like one of the potted palms, a little more functional perhaps. Whereas for me, it was a temporary thing, a bridge between my freshman and sophomore years at LSU. Then, after I graduated, I was planning on veterinary school. And unlike Carl, I'd fuck any color of boy, had fucked every color of boy.

This kid we were talking about had that Kennedy look, if you know what I mean: tousled fair hair and a clear complexion, his eyes bright blue and eager. He was very short, standing only about five-four, five-five. His clothes were stylish: blazer jacket and silk rep tie, tan khaki pants with a web belt, woven ducks flying around his thin waist, and highly polished penny loafers. Brooks Brothers.

I scooped up his family's expensive, monogrammed luggage, stacked it neatly on the cart, and hung the three-suiters on the bar.

"Watch you don't muss them," the woman haughtily commanded. "My gowns."

While we were waiting for the elevators, the piss-elegant woman said to her husband, "I am simply *staaved, Chaals* . May we dine right away?" I didn't think anybody actually talked like that. She had an unmistakable English accent, uppercrust, but somehow kind of phony.

"You folks English?" I politely asked.

"Australian," the man responded. "From Sydney." The way he said it made me feel like I'd insulted him. He sort of stood a little straighter and averted his head as if he was not accustomed to being addressed by the help. I'll confess, when I encountered this type at the hotel, I started to share Carl's antagonisms.

"Your hair is mussed, Chaals," the woman said, this time to her son as she brushed back a thick coil. I assumed he was Charlie Junior.

Cute little "Chaals" had been sneaking surreptitious glances at me from the moment I'd first approached the party. I wasn't conceited enough to think there may have been some interest there. I figured it was more like I was the first black man he'd been that close to. I was well aware of the immigration restrictions in their native country.

The elevator arrived and I ushered them inside, backing in with the luggage cart. Junior was just behind me against the wall. They were on the sixteenth floor, our highest, where the most expensive suites were located. A fancy rooftop restaurant had been added above that, so the elevator began to fill with swells headed in that direction. I was pressed further and further to the rear. Against Charlie Junior.

Against Charlie Junior's groin. Against Charlie Junior's hard-on.

Without a doubt, the boy was boned up and pressing his dick into my ass. The elevator stopped again. More people tried to get on. Using the pretext of shifting to accommodate them, I verified the erection. Reaching around behind me, on the side away from the seniors, I felt Junior's cock. It was folded in a large lump, and I couldn't tell how big it was, but the bulge was firm and unyielding. He pressed it against my palm. The boy was hot. I actually leaned against him and he returned the pressure. I erected on the instant. Then the boy brazenly slid his hand between my thighs and I pressed them together. I felt like creaming as he rubbed my balls.

The elevator arrived at their floor, and I reluctantly maneuvered us out of the crowded confines. Charlie Junior walked behind his parents as I preceded them down the hall. I unlocked their door and went through the routine of installing them in their suite. With mounting interest, I noticed that little Charlie's room was securely separate. He motioned me to carry his luggage in there. We were momentarily obscured by the half-ajar connecting door.

Since this is an older hotel, the rooms have separate air conditioners, and the maid had neglected to turn Charlie's on. I went over to correct the oversight, and Charlie ostensibly went to pee in the bathroom beside the window unit. He didn't close the door. He stood sideways at the toilet and pulled out his dick. It was still hard as a fist. He stared at me. I stared at him. He stared at my groin. I stared at his dick. My hands shook as I fumbled with the controls.

From the other room, I heard the couple planning to go upstairs for lunch. If I didn't get the hell out of there right away, they'd find me down on my knees sucking on their son's meat. I gave him one last, forlorn, agonized glance and was rewarded to see his disappointment draw down his fine features. I shrugged my shoulders and mouthed the words, "Not now."

When Charles Senior plunked two quarters into my palm, I stared at it in disbelief.

"No shit!" Carl said when I told him what had happened. "Some guys have all the luck." He meant it both ways, a little sarcasm mixed with envy.

"Thought you didn't like vanilla?"

"Pretty little thing like that? Go on, Joey."

"Glad you're coming to your senses," I told him.

My shift didn't end until seven, and it was only two o'clock then. I didn't know how I was going to hold out for the next few hours. The only problem I really had to deal with was the hotel rule about not fraternizing with the patrons. Little Charlie was resourceful, though. I guessed he'd been around the block a few times. About an hour before my shift ended, the bell captain came over to our station.

"The college kid in 1602 wants to be a mystery writer," he said. "He wants to get a feel for hotel workers. Go up and talk to him at the end of your shift, Joey. He asked for the guy who handled their bags."

Carl nudged me and I tried to keep a straight face as I said okay.

I didn't change out of my black pants and red monkey suit, nor my red bellman's cap that makes me look like I have a flat head. I was swooshed to the sixteenth floor a little after seven. Number two was the kid's side of the suite, and I rapped softly on his door. He answered it wearing a pair of wrinkled cotton shorts. He was barefoot.

He didn't say a word but motioned me inside. Instead of falling on the bed and fucking our brains out, as I'd been eagerly anticipating, Charlie sat in an easy chair and directed me in front of him.

"Pull down your pants," he said, speaking in that English accent for the first time. There was an imperious tone to his voice that didn't sit all that well with me. Mentally shrugging "what the hell," I unfastened my fly and slid the uniform and my underwear down to just above my knees. Then I held my arms out just a little and let him look at me. My cock was half-hard and swung to one side. It began to lengthen under his steady appraisal. "You'll do," he said at length.

"I'll *do*?" I asked him, incredulous.

Talk about pissing me off! Charlie was looking at me like I was a slab of meat in the butcher's shop, trying to decide if he wanted to buy it or not. Carl had been right on the money when he surmised where this little sucker was coming from. "I'll do," indeed!

"I think not," I said, beginning to pull up my pants.

My earlier attraction to him receded completely. For all his cute good looks, I wanted to be more than a casual trinket he could play with while here in New Orleans.

His lips protruded in a pout, a hurt-little-boy look, making him cute as hell, but turning me off completely. When Charlie saw that I was seriously intent on leaving, he jumped off his chair and blocked the door.

"I'll pay you," he said.

Talk about knowing exactly the wrong thing to say! My dad had always said I was too "prideful"—his word—for my own good. I straightened my jacket with a defiant snap and said unkindly, "Buy yourself another boy—plenty of 'em down in the French Quarter."

"I'm not allowed out," he said with a pout.

"Not my problem, little buddy."

"Everywhere else we go, they do," he stated with conviction. "Any bellboy I ask."

"Well, I ain't just any bellboy, and I don't."

"Aren't. You *aren't* just any bellboy," he said spitefully.

"Why you little shit!" I spat. I had to restrain my fist to keep from slugging him.

"I suck cock good," he asserted with an upward jerk of his chin.

"Not this cock!" I shoved him rudely aside, and he fell against the door jamb. He slumped to the floor. I got my hand on the knob, but his shoulder was wedged against the door. "Let me out," I said warningly.

He grabbed hold of my leg at the calf. "Please," he pleaded.

"Fuck off!" I hissed, tearing my leg from his grasp.

And then, the little bastard started crying.

His eyes scrunched up and real tears rolled down his smooth young cheeks. His shoulders heaved piteously, and he slumped his head to his chest. He scooted out of the way of the door and didn't look at me. I stood above him, not certain if I hated him or just felt sorry for him. Then his head came up and he looked at me with those blue, blue eyes from which tears were now streaming.

"I'm sorry," he sniffled.

Aw shit! I melted.

Suddenly, I could see his life: dragged halfway around the world by two supercilious and self-centered monsters for parents, probably given no attention save for money, anything he wanted coming easy, bought. An accident of birth determines who our parents are, our color, our class. . .It suddenly dawned on me that this lonely kid was as powerless to change his circumstances as Carl was.

I dropped to my knees and lifted his face by the chin. "C'mon, little guy," I whispered. "Don't cry."

He averted his face and sobbed harder. His thin shoulders were shaking, and I held him to me. At first he resisted, pulling back. Then I felt him going slack in my arms. If the kid were acting, he'd win the Oscar. His shudders stilled and he wiped his eyes with the back of his hand.

"It's all shit," he said.

"No," I said, patting his shoulder. "It is not." I kissed away the salty tears from his lashes.

He laid his head sideways on my chest, and I hugged him tightly. "What's your name?" he asked so softly I could barely hear him.

"Joey," I whispered in his ear, licking the words in.

My hormones kicked into high gear as I felt his body against mine. It started innocently enough, me lightly brushing his forehead with little kisses, him leaning into my embrace more fully. He snuggled under my chin and wrapped his arms around my chest, pulled me close. He lay very still and I stroked his back. Our mouths came together. His tongue darted between my lips.

All of a sudden, he was all over me, pushing my cap off with a hard caress beginning at my brow, then back onto my head, my neck, pulling my face against his, kissing me deeply and squirming in my arms like a warm puppy. His hands fluttered across my chest like demented butterflies, snaking inside the buttons of my jacket, snapping them open and moving heatedly over my pecs.

We spread full length on the floor, and Charlie was all arms and wetness and tight little hollows which were moist with his sweat. I climbed on top of his half-naked body and reveled in the feel of him. I licked his pits till the long golden hairs were trailing to his heaving sides. I sucked on his nipples till they were thick and hard. The mound in his shorts grew larger, and he pressed his cock tightly against my groin and rutted into me, bucking his flanks into the friction.

Charlie yanked off my jacket and shirt. He practically tore my pants in half as he grappled me out of them. I pulled down his shorts to just his underwear. And then the kid got playful. He wriggled out of his Calvins and pulled them over my head. He positioned the crotch at my mouth and opened the fly. He kissed me through the thin white fabric and sucked my tongue out the gap. I extended my tongue to its full length, and he sucked it like a stiff cock hanging out of the fly, mouthing up and down with little whimpers and sighs.

Naked, he was all male, a tightly bound coil of electricity, unwound and writhing in my arms. His buttocks were firm and supple, and I kneaded them in turn, palming over the smooth curves of his sweet melons. His crack was moist and dewy. I kept one hand cleaved up between his cheeks and stroked his stiff cock.

His meat was above average size, truthfully, about the same as mine. He was clean and clipped. I stroked his joint between our pressed bellies. Then I held our cocks tightly together and stroked the combined fatness. Lube juice drooled out of our joined knobs and smeared our slickened flesh.

Charlie was light and compliant when I lifted him and carried him to the bed. I placed him on his back and fell on top of him. I wanted to touch, feel, smell, lick, taste, and eat every patch of him from head to toe. So I did. Kneeling between his legs, I licked the soles of his feet and sucked on his toes, each one independently. Then I worked my way up his legs, washing the insides of his thighs, up to his crotch and into his ass. Charlie spread his legs and lifted them in the air by his knees.

Charlie's pucker was succulent and tart, and I licked over the hotter flesh several times before reaming in. He sighed contentedly as my tongue speared up his flexing chute. He clenched his butt tightly, then relaxed, opening his tunnel for my penetration. He jacked himself as I hungrily ate him out. Charlie trembled and quivered as I hungrily lapped at his bittersweet hole. I wanted to fuck this boy like I'd never fucked another. He pushed back against my feeding face, and I ate even more ravenously at his funk.

Eating ass is so intoxicating to me that I almost came on him then. Reaming makes my pre-cum drool in anticipation, and right then, lube juice was flowing like a leaking faucet, oozing out of my cockhead and dripping to the sheets.

I pulled off his slickened ass and trailed my tongue up the little ridge of skin that led to the base of his cock. I licked and sucked on his balls till they drew up tightly in their sac. The cloying smell of his sex was overwhelming, delicious. He dropped his legs around my shoulders and I sucked his cock.Charlie put a hand on each side of my face and his fingers enclosed my mouth as I went down on him all the way to his balls. I felt his cock muscle-jerking like he was getting ready to come, and I drew off, sucked back to just the head and looked up at him.

His bright eyes were teasing now, coy and lustful at the same time. "Fuck me, Joey," he said in a lewd whisper.

I lifted his buttocks by the base of his spine, and he arched his back to give me his ass. I brought the knob of my cock up to his pucker and teased him with the flaring head. He was still juicy from my spit. I wedged my cockhead against his rose and pushed my knob into his ass-ring.

"Ah! Ah! Ah!" Joey panted as I started working my meat inside him. His assflesh was soft and yielding, velvety and warm. It was all I could do to hold back from shoving right in. But I held the crown of my rigid tool just inside his pucker till he grew accustomed to the girth filling him. Then I started slowly pressing in.

"Oh, yeah! Ah, yeah!" I grunted. "Take my fuck, baby. Take that cock!"

"Easy, mate. Go up me easy," Joey said between clenched teeth. His eyes were slitted up and his pretty mouth was wet. I slid my tongue inside his lips with a slow, measured thrust, matching the slow thrust of my cock entering his ass. "Uh! Uh! Uh!" he panted inside my mouth.

I rode his backside up further, bent him near double, and pushed in all the way. I drew back and watched him as he took all my meat. "Good, baby. So—damn—good," I groaned. "Sweet, sweet ass!"

"Yes! Yes! Yes!" he moaned.

I grabbed his cock and started jacking him off in a slow, pumping rhythm in time with my thrusting strokes. "Get it, baby, get it!" I harshly whispered. "Take my fuck, baby! Take it!"

"Ah, yeah!" he grunted. "Fuck me, Joey! Fuck me!"

My cock slid in and out of his chute like the piston of a revving engine. I gyrated my pelvis frantically and scoured his ass-walls. It felt like I was in a smooth velvet vise and the kid's ass-muscles were milking me off. It was delirious and wild, like ravenous animals coupling.

I held him in a tight embrace to cushion him against the fury of my frenzied fuck. The sound of my pelvis slapping his assflesh was intoxicating. Charlie spread his legs wide, hunched back further onto my root, and I banged away inside his guts, pounding my balls hard into the trench of his ass. Such delirious ecstasy couldn't last very long.

"I'm gonna come!" Charlie yelped.

I jacked him harder and faster. I felt his cock pulsing with racing cream which rushed up his tube and spurted out all over his belly. Three long cock-shots of his spunk barreled out and ran in streaming rivulets down his sides. A streaming rope of dick-gravy splattered onto his face. That sight brought me off.

Quivering and shaking like I was having a fit, I blew my nuts up Charlie's hole. He reached around and held me tightly to his rump as I unloaded what felt like buckets of cum up his ass. It was all we could do to keep my balance as my violent discharge pumped into him. I was tortured on the rack of his body.

I went rigid all over and drained all the sauce from my nuts. Then I fell, spent and exhausted, on top of him. I cradled his head into the hollow of my shoulder and stroked his sweaty hair.

"You're right, Joey," he mumbled into my neck. "You ain't just any bell boy."

It took a great deal of persuasion to convince Charlie's father to let his son out for a night on the town. Seems they were afraid of him being kidnapped and held for ransom. So they signed me on as a part-time bodyguard. They were there for three nights, and I spent each one with Charlie. Charles Senior gave me a hefty tip when they checked out, but it was nothing compared to what Junior had given me. He promised I'd see him again and I have a feeling it's a promise he'll keep.

TRASHMEN

❖ ❖ ❖

In the stifling heat of the murky warehouse, their hot, sweaty torsos slid wetly along the entire length of my straining body. . .I wanted to fuck them so much that I wished I could double myself. . . But these guys had other ideas.

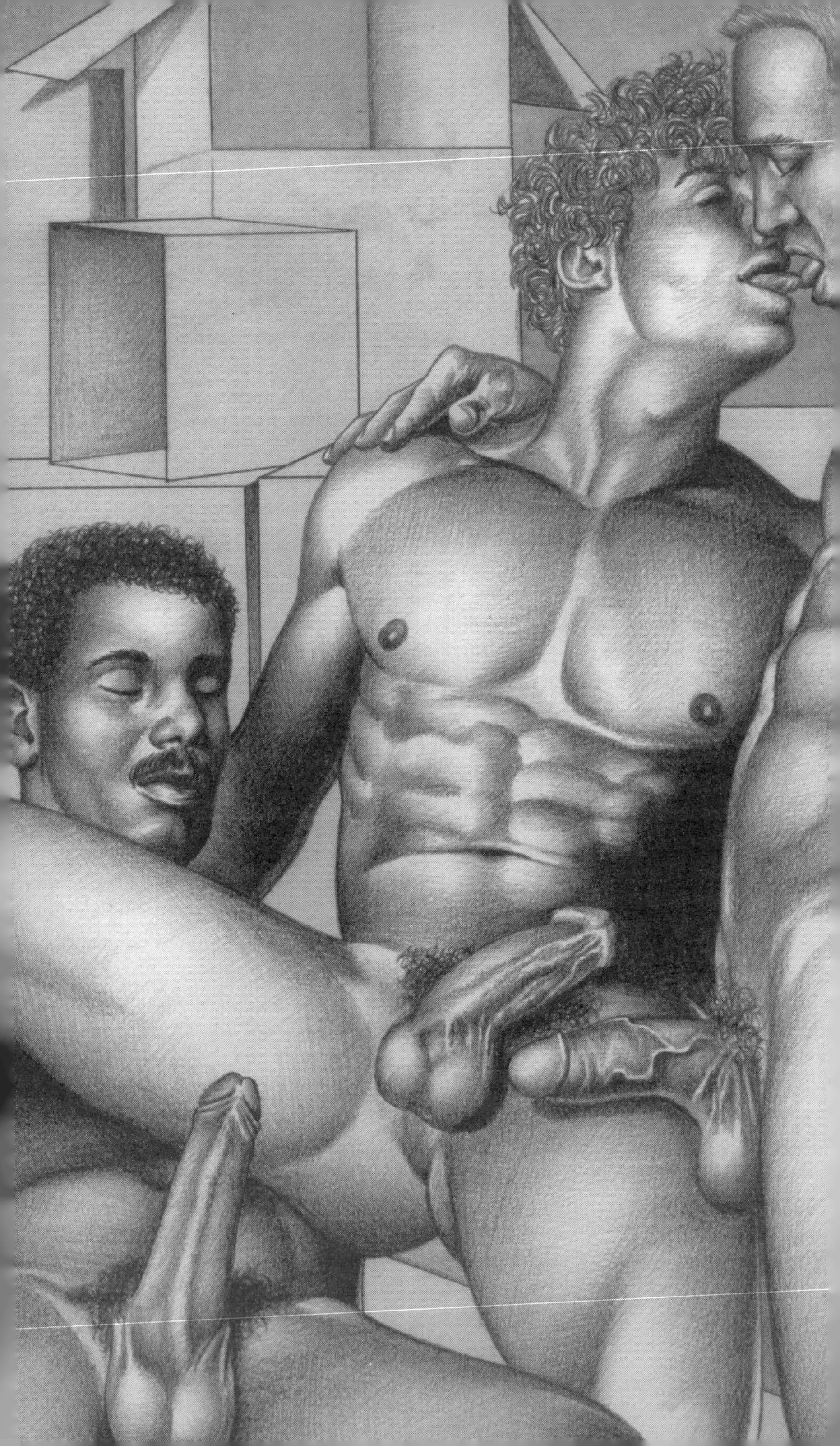

Trashmen

Acquiring and collecting porno magazines has been my hobby for years. I had been buying them since I was eighteen, and that was ten years ago. So, by the time I was preparing to move from Florida to New Orleans, I had a pretty good supply, hundreds in fact. Some of the pages in my favorites were so badly stuck together with cum-glue that they were nearly illegible.

These I decided to discard before I started packing. That's when I began to think about how to get rid of them—not so easy. I didn't exactly relish the idea of offering cum-smeared fuck books to my friends. In any event, most of them have videos, which several have told me they prefer over the written word and still shots of hot models.

"Whatever blows your skirt up," I'd told them in the past.

I was moving my few personal belongings in my ancient Volkswagen Beetle, so I was limited in what I could take. By the time I'd sorted through the books (with a brief intermission to masturbate as I reread a hot orgy scene), I had a large pile to get rid of, over half of them. Now I had to figure out how to dispose of them without "corrupting" any passers-by who might be puritanical or so lacking in taste that they couldn't appreciate an exquisite naked guy with a big erect cock. Go figure.

I couldn't just dump them on the trash pile in front of my apartment for a minor or a straight neighbor to possibly pick over. Maybe if I wrapped them in several large black garbage bags and dumped them into a dumpster somewhere? No, derelicts are always rummaging through those and might scatter them around.

Here in Miami it's against the law to burn anything, so that was out of the question. How about sneaking them out to the curb under some filthy garbage? Uh-uh, derelicts again. Besides, it would be like tossing old loves out with the smelly refuse.

I sat there in a quandary, knowing I had to do something that night because I had to be on the road as soon as I finished my last day at the office tomorrow. I considered the possibility of just abandoning the magazines in my apartment but rejected that idea as I respected my landlady and wouldn't want to shock her. Shit!

After ruminating over half a dozen possible solutions to my dilemma, I decided to wake up very early the next morning and personally hand them over to the trashmen who always come before sunup. Accordingly, I packed up the magazines, sealed them tightly with silver duct tape and went to bed, setting my alarm for 4:30 A.M.

When the damned thing jangled me awake at that hour, it felt like the middle of the night. I climbed out of bed bleary-eyed and confused, until I remembered my chore. I went to the bathroom and pissed away my hard-on. Then I pulled on a pair of worn-out jeans and hefted the box in my fairly strong arms. It was a struggle lugging the weight downstairs, but I made it with much huffing and puffing, sweating with the effort. Summer in Miami.

I paused on the dark street outside, rested the heavy carton on the stoop, and caught my breath. A thick blanket of fog roiled around me. I heard the trash truck rumbling and screeching about two or three blocks away, so I shouldered the burdensome container and half dragged it to the curb underneath the street lamp.

I looked fearfully back up at the apartment house, thinking that anyone observing me would find it peculiar, perhaps more than a little odd that I should be up to hand-deliver my garbage at that ungodly hour of the morning.

"Oh, what the hell, I'm moving anyway," I thought. I sat on my secret treasures among my neighbor's deposits and guarded them in the halo of fog and light.

Presently, the big open dump truck lumbered around the corner and stabbed me with its headlight beams. I stood and waited till it ground to a stop at the curb beside me.

TRASHMEN

As they opened the door and swung down out of the cab, I saw that only two hunky guys were manning the trash collection. And what a sight! One gleaming black bruiser and a slighter and younger white guy, both of them shirtless, walked toward me. The black guy had a quizzical look on his broad, friendly face, and appeared to be in his middle thirties. His bare torso gave new definition to well-muscled. His massive pectorals glistened with sweat which ran in rivulets over his hard, flat belly. He must've been six-feet-two.

The white man in his mid-twenties was trimmer, though still magnificently proportioned. Clad only in tight jeans and heavy brown work boots, he was the very picture of rugged masculine beauty. His close-cropped hair shone golden under the orange street light, his eyes a quick, bright blue.

I gazed at them in fascination as they approached.

"Up pretty early," the black guy observed as they stood in front of me. And it was true. I'd thrown a helluva bone watching the crotches of the handsome men as they'd swaggered toward me. They both had delicious-looking bulges straining in their pants.

"Or out kinda late," the white stud commented.

"Both," I said, not elaborating.

I watched as they began unceremoniously picking up the rubbish and effortlessly tossing it into the bed of the truck. Their rippling muscles worked in perfect unison, broad shoulders glinting with sweat as they strained to the task. Both men's backs were hard and well-planed. Their asses, round as ripe melons, stood out as the fabric of their tight pants cleaved their cracks when they bent over.

I caught my breath for a second as the younger guy lifted the box containing my cummed-up fuck books.

"What if it breaks open and they fall out?" I thought.

But it didn't and he threw it nonchalantly onto the growing heap. I stood rooted to the spot until they finished.

"Thanks," I mumbled weakly, for I hated to see them leave.

My boner strained against my Levi's as the kid waved, smiled brightly, and said, "So long."

"See you, man," his partner shouted from the open window as they took off.

I trudged back up to my forlornly empty apartment with my raging hard-on dripping lube juice like a sieve. I decided to pound my meat since it was still early in the morning, still dark. I got out one of my remaining fuck books and turned to a hot picture of one guy taking it up the butt while another ate his meat. The first guy was bent over a table, the top man ramming his horsecock home, and the third was feeding on a long-shafted prick from beneath the table. Since this book was old, it showed cum running out of the guy's mouth, a real collector's item.

I started reading a hot story about two ranch hands and was working myself up pretty close to coming when I heard a noise outside my open window. It was the dump truck; I just knew it! I raced to the window and looked down.

Sure enough, it was. But only the black guy was in it. He'd pulled the truck just inside the ring of light, a little back from where I was fast going into a frenzy. I could see down through the windshield that his pants were down around his ankles and he was shafting his tremendous hammer-headed cock. A few times, he took his monstrous, purple-crowned joystick and beat it against the steering wheel. The flaring, uncut knob grew more purple, almost crimson, and the heavy fucker glistened with wetness in the soft, orange light.

I could see my discarded fuck books scattered all over the seat of the truck; many had fallen to the floor. He seemed oblivious to my watching him and fisted himself harder, looking through the books. I grew delirious with pleasure just watching. Presently, he raised his head and scanned the facade of my apartment building, eventually settling on my lighted window. His eyes found mine. He smiled broadly. He motioned for me to come down. No power on earth could have prevented me from racing to my closet, skimming into my jeans and darting down the stairs two at a time.

My legs shook as I approached the truck and cautiously peered in. He grinned wickedly and asked in a throaty voice, "Like cock, huh?"

"God, yes!" My voice was ragged.

He held his huge horsecock out for display, squeezing his yielding cockflesh at the fat base of his heavily veined shaft. The gorgeous mushroom head leaked pre-cum over the deep, velvety folds of dickskin, forming a dark nozzle at the bulbous head. He splayed his legs open for my inspection of this choicest slab of cockflesh I'd seen in ages.

"Get in," he said in the same gruff manner.

I reached through the window and grabbed his fat cock.

"Ah yeah!" he said lewdly.

I was shaking with excitement and nervousness as I circled the truck and climbed in beside him, shoving the remaining cum-smeared fuck books to the floor.

"What if this is a trap?" flew through my mind.

I reached over and grabbed his cock again and squeezed it hard. He said nothing, but cranked up the truck and we roared off.

"What if he's taking me somewhere so he and his buddy can beat me up, rob me? What if these butch hunks like to kill queers for an early morning exercise?" Scared as I was, my rod tented up my jeans until the copper buttons of the 501's strained to contain the whole thing.

"God, what I won't risk for fresh dick!" I thought, as he swerved the truck down a dark, deserted alley and skidded to a stop before a derelict warehouse.

The big man spoke for the first time, as he tugged his khaki pants over his still-swollen erection. "My name's Clayton, son, what's yours?"

Terrified, I timorously said, "Tony." Said it so quickly, it was almost a monosyllable. It was deathly still as we climbed from the cab.

Clayton came quickly around the truck and walked up to a corrugated metal door that was bent deeply in the middle. It wasn't locked, and he pulled it open with a scraping noise that set my nerves on edge. He motioned me inside, and I followed my stiff prick into the darkness. He closed the door.

After my eyes adjusted to the dim interior, I made out a rubble-strewn area in the vastness of the warehouse. Clayton took me roughly by the hand, and I debated whether I should make a break for it. This might be my only chance to shake loose and light out running for the front door. I'm in good shape and figured I could get away from him.

But he propelled me along with deliberate steps, making for a secluded area behind a pile of empty cardboard boxes. When we came around behind them, I almost lost my balance. There, on a bare double mattress, lay the other trash collector. And he was buck naked!

"This is Kenny," Clayton said. "He's the one that collects the good junk some people toss out."

"Yeah! Good junk," the nude guy on the mattress said in a low, sexy tone. Some more of my fuck books were scattered on the floor around the mattress. Kenny grasped his blood-engorged cock in his fist and pointed the huge thing at me. "Were they his?" he asked Clayton.

"Yeah," Clayton said. "You were right." Then to me, he said, "Get naked, man."

He burst open the button of his pants, viciously zipped down his fly, and hurriedly pushed his underwear and all down to his ankles in a single swipe. My legs were near buckling from fear and excitement as I saw his dripping cock begin to rear its flaring head again. His creambag hung low beneath the veiny shaft and his bull-balls swung as he stepped out of his clothes.

"C'mon, man," he growled throatily as I hesitated. "Strip!"

Kenny on the mattress reached up and fondled me in the groin. "Yeah, man, hurry," he said as he stroked the folded lump in my swollen crotch.

I shucked out of my jeans and Calvins, and Clayton immediately grabbed me from behind and pulled me onto the bare mattress. It was rough and stained with what must have been buckets of shot-off cum, smelling musky and faintly sweetish. I fell between the two butch men and lay flat on my back. Surprisingly, the three of us kissed, sloppily tonguing whichever lips we encountered in the near-dark. I held their two erections, one in each hand, and fisted them up to their fullest length, each long delectable cock webbing my fingers with penile saliva.

In the stifling heat of the murky warehouse, their hot, sweaty torsos slid wetly along the entire length of my straining body. The smell of hot sexflesh filled the tight confines as we groped and grappled at one another. They took turns shafting my jutting pole so that one hand of each glided up and down its stretching length in tandem. I felt like I was going to come any minute as they worked on me.

I wanted to fuck them so much that I wished I could double myself so I wouldn't have to choose which one first. But these guys had other ideas.

Clayton suddenly left off feeding on my feverish lips with his fleshy ones and reversed himself, his dark puckered asshole pressing into my face. I palmed his cheeks apart and licked at his bittersweet musk. He sucked on my throbbing root while Kenny moved his head down and suckled at my cum-filled balls. I was already delirious with pleasure when Kenny hiked my ass up a little and started eating his way into my hole, tongue-fucking me deeply while Clayton sheathed my spit-slickened dick with his hot working mouth. His soft lips felt like I'd gotten my cock into a milking furnace.

My nuts boiled and all I could feel was heat—heat from their sweaty bodies, more heat on my thick, aching prick, and a burning sensation at my butthole. I threw my arms to each side and lay there moaning and nearly crying from the tormenting pleasure. My body trembled and was wracked with lightning-like sensations rippling over the raw nerves of my skin.

Suddenly, Kenny stopped his slobbering at my hole, and Clayton again reversed his position, bringing his beautiful black face up to mine, and we kissed. He embraced me and rolled me on top of him. Since he was on the bottom, I thought he was ready for the fuck I was dying to give him.

But no. Instead, I looked over my shoulder and saw Kenny slip a rubber over Clayton's monster cock and guide the fat knob up to my slobber-filled hole. I'd never really enjoyed being fucked before but figured, "What the hell." My buttchute was already hanging open from the tongue-fuck that Kenny had given me, so I relaxed onto Clayton's fucklog as easily as I could manage, considering the size of the bloated organ.

His heavy slab of meat slid inside my ass-ring and he hunched his way half into me. Kenny assisted with his mouth as he drooled over Clayton's big cock, licking and slurping around its fleshy length as he penetrated me further. God, but he was big! He pushed into my yielding assflesh, strained my channel wide open and started pumping his meat to me. We deep-tongued each other's mouth, and I felt a new sensation. Kenny was at my backside, sliding his tongue into me at the same time that Clayton's cock shoved in and out of my prick-filled hole.

Then Kenny stopped swabbing my crack and climbed onto my back, his swollen root pressing against my assflesh, me a sandwich between the two big men.

"Fuck 'im, Clayton! Fuck 'im good," Kenny panted. He slid his rock-hard body all over my sweaty and heaving back as Clayton hunched his hard ass up and down, fucking into me more deeply than I'd ever been fucked. Kenny kept on. "That's it! Feed it to 'im, man. Give 'im that hot cock. Deep-dick that fucker!"

Clayton groaned and moaned, and we continued to kiss wildly. Kenny hunkered down with my cock-filled butt between his thighs, his huge prod pressing up against my cock-stretched bunghole, which was filled to the limit with Clayton's grinding fuckmeat. Kenny took his and Clayton's slippery cocks and held them together as Clayton's slid in and out of my tortured rectum. Clayton's loins stopped grinding and he pulled his shaft nearly out of me, just the full crown remaining within, held tightly by my pucker.

And then I got the idea when I felt Kenny push tentatively at my hole with his slimy cock. There was no way! It was impossible! They both wanted to fuck me at the same time! I couldn't get *both* their tremendous poles up my butt!

Clayton held me tighter than ever in his big firm arms. "C'mon, c'mon, c'mon," he whispered wetly into my ear, tonguing the words in, his fuck held fast in my ass. "You can take it, man. You can do it. C'mon, get Kenny too, baby. Get 'im off with both of us inside you."

I felt myself splitting then as Kenny guided both their thick cocks up and into my dripping hole. My legs splayed open and I gasped with pain as the two men entered me, fucking me from below and on top. Kenny pressed his weight onto my back, driving his throbbing rod further into my ass as they ground me between them. I felt both their slippery cocks up and down the other's length, pistoning in and out of my ass in alternating strokes.

The pain subsided and I went into an ecstasy of passion as the two men worked their cocks together, spearing my chute wider than I would've thought possible. My cock was near to bursting as their rocking fuck pressed it between Clayton's flat belly and mine. Kenny held Clayton and myself in a death grip as he ball-slapped his way into me. Clayton pulled Kenny's fuck deeper inside of me, jabbing at my trigger and making my cum boil. They moaned like they were fixing to come.

I felt my own egg-juice start gushing up and out of my squashed nuts, up my inflamed cock squeezed tightly between our straining bellies. Clayton and Kenny increased the tempo of their joint fuck, pounding their meat faster and faster into my guts and driving me over the edge, igniting my sparkplug till paroxysms of torturous ecstasy thundered between us.

They panted and heaved, gibbered and slobbered, moans of pleasure escaping their gasping breaths as they began to cream off at the same time.

Kenny reared back, slapped his calloused hands onto my spine and nearly shouted, "Here it comes, baby! Get yours!"

Clayton moaned, "Yeah! Yeah! Yeah! I'm coming, man. Get it!

Take it, man, take it!"

With that, they pulled out, skinned off the rubbers, and kneeled next to each other, Clayton holding their exploding cocks together in two hands. Punching out their hips, they blasted their twin eruptions all over me. Copious buckets of manseed, shot after shot of arching milk spewed in streams and spurting fountains. They shot so much cum, I could feel it running in rivulets down my quaking body, twin rivers of milky froth ejected down the lengths of their pressed together pricks, squishing our sexflesh together with cum-glue.

My cum sprayed out my pisshole in bursting wads, pumping out more milk than it had ever done before. My spunk felt like it was hitting the ceiling. I thought I was going to die from the convulsive spasm that shuddered throughout my entire midsection.

The smells of sex and sweat and cum filled the air. My asshole felt torn wide open. My lungs burst with pleasure. My cock kept shooting off geysers of juice, splattering on their chests and bellies, giving their genitals a fresh bath of dick-sauce. I thought I'd been fucked to death and this was heaven. There was nothing but cock in my head and cock all over me, cock and more cock, cum and more cum.

They fell to each side of me, and I held them pressed tightly to me. I kissed each one deeply in turn and they snuggled against me.

Full dawn had broken and a gray light shone dimly through the grimy windows. As my breathing returned to normal, I rose shakily to my feet and began to gather up my scattered clothes.

"Stay with us, Tony," Kenny said. "The hell with the rest of our route."

"But you guys don't live here, do you?" I asked.

"Hell no. We're both married," Clayton said with a chuckle. "But a guy's gotta have a little fun on the long night shift. We're just friendly partners. That right, Kenny?" With that, the black man teasingly tousled Kenny's short hair.

And so I stayed with them for the rest of that day. If folks in Miami were pissed off because they didn't get their trash picked up that day, I guess they should talk to their trashmen about it. They're real friendly guys, once you get to know them.

LUKE'S DADDY

❖ ❖ ❖

Dane pulled his cock and balls out of the jockstrap, and the elastic pushed the whole dark mass of his genitals into his stomach. It was just as Luke had described; the black man's root tasted spicy and funky...

Luke's Daddy

Luke Summers is the most brazen and cock-hungry guy I know. He's farm-boy pretty—that's the only way I can describe him. You can almost visualize a stalk of oats hanging out of his pretty lips. I use that word advisedly. His lips are *pretty*, moist and full. He has a cowlick right in front of his short, blond hair, and his eyes are a robin's egg blue. He's nineteen and butch as hell, even if he is pretty.

Luke will do absolutely anything to get his rocks off and as many times as possible. The boy is insatiable. The dirtier the sex, the better he likes it—hot, sweaty man-sex. I've never heard Luke call anything kinky. He's into getting it on with straight guys, gay guys, butches, fems. Doesn't matter—anything, so long as it's male. Uniforms turn him on. One day he's an exhibitionist, the next a voyeur. He loves to be pissed on and he loves to drink it. He loves a little S & M thrown in. Any kind of fantasy gets his juices flowing. And, being one himself, he certainly knows how to pleasure a man.

The little fucker's got a big, long one, like some smaller men do, their heavy cocks making up for their short stature. And one of the prettiest little butts you've ever seen. He has one of those asses which is high-hung, fairly jumping off his spine in twin mounds of assflesh with a deep ditch, making his little melons just ripe for fucking.

He told me that when I wasn't around serving as his cum-catcher, he would sit on this low wall outside of the park here in the small

Tennessee community we both live in, with his big cock and balls hanging out of a hole he had ripped open in the crotch of his Levi's. He'd cruise the cars passing by, and if a single man was in it alone, Luke would move his hand to the side so the dude could see his genitals. He got beaten up a couple of times for exposing himself that way, but that didn't slow him down a bit.

"If they're looking down there anyway, they must be looking for something," he'd said.

Then, if the guy circled the block a couple of times, Luke would get hard and keep his huge rod between his legs, but then let the guy see it when he passed. I've watched Luke do this a couple of times when he didn't know I was looking. What Luke didn't realize was that his balls are so big, anybody could have seen them hanging in their creambag from between his thighs as they approached. His nuts look like furry tomatoes.

Luke has a mania for public toilets. I think the chance of getting caught turns him on as well. Anything dangerous or risky is right up Luke's alley, his butt-alley usually.

I'm twenty-five and often think of Luke as my gay son. My name is Ben Saxon and I'm on the road a lot, having the eastern half of Tennessee as my territory. I had found a promising public bathroom last week and taken Luke there, as I often do, knowing his mania for such places. He'd sucked off two truckers through the glory holes and a big black driver who was staying in the motel out back. I had lost count after that. The black man had said he had to make a drop-off and gas up, but to meet him in number three in two hours.

"You're obsessed, Luke," I said. "How could you possibly get off again?"

"'Cause I'm young, hung, and full of cum," he said, one of his favorite expressions.

"You've got too much sap in you, you little bugger." That was my nickname for him and I used it affectionately. "The guy said two hours and it isn't even dark yet. We can't hang around here until then."

"I want you to taste that black man's meat, Ben. It was good."

"How can you remember what one guy's dick tastes like? Jeez, Luke, you did three or four."

"Because it was spicy—tasted like cinnamon or nutmeg, Christmas flavored."

"C'mon then, let's go," I said. "We'll kill the time in the cafe."

❖

The rooms the truck stop had for rent in back of the restaurant and service station reminded me of cheap motels built in the Fifties. Two lengthy concrete buildings were joined to form an L-shaped structure which stood detached from the main building. We located number three and Luke rapped lightly on the red painted door.

"Come in," we heard the black driver say from inside the room.

Luke pushed through the door and I followed. The room was a tiny cubicle, with barely enough room to change your mind in. Since the drivers used them principally as a place to nap, the rooms were minimally furnished with a double bed and one small night stand. The black guy was lying on the bed.

Clad only in a jockstrap, he was leafing through a skin magazine, with a pile of several beside him. He was only half-tumescent, but his cock bulged in the pouch like a folded lump of sausage. He palmed his warm brown hand over his crotch and smiled at us.

"I've been waiting for you, pretty boy," he said to Luke. To me, "My name's Dane. What's yours?"

I told him Ben, and he said matter-of-factly, "Get naked, Ben. Let's have some fun."

Luke and I started stripping under Dane's hungry gaze. His cock lengthened as he watched us.

"Leave your underwear on," Dane said after we'd shed our jeans. "So this is your son, huh?"

It was as if this handsome hunk had read my mind about the way I feel for Luke. I went blank for only a moment, then I knew how to play it.

"Yeah," I said gruffly, "this is Luke. He's my little boy."

"Did you teach him how to suck cock?" Dane slurred lasciviously.

"Yeah," I said in a low, dirty way.

"Well, you didn't teach him very good," Dane said. "He damned near bit my cock off back in the toilets."

I looked sternly at Luke. "Is that so, Son? You didn't suck the man's cock like I taught you to?"

Luke put a hangdog expression on his face and said sheepishly, "It was too big, Daddy. I couldn't hardly get my mouth around it. I did the best I could."

From the bed, Dane growled, "I think you ought to beat his little butt for that. Teach him how to suck a man's dick like he should."

"Yeah, I think I'm gonna have to do that," I said, glowering menacingly at Luke. "C'mon Son, get over my lap. Daddy's going to have to spank you. Do you want Daddy to spank you?"

"No, Daddy," Luke said in an adolescent voice. "Please don't spank me. I'll try harder."

I sat on the edge of the bed next to Dane. "Get over here, Son, I have to punish you. Then I'll have to teach you how to suck cock all over again. Come here."

Luke walked warily to the side of the bed, and I grabbed him and threw him forcefully across my thighs. His cock was already hard and dug into my groin. My boner leapt to attention. I shoved his ass, pushing him harder onto my lap, and my cockhead slid out of the waistband of my Jockeys.

"Hold his head, man," I said to Dane, "while I beat his little ass."

Luke wriggled and squirmed like a puppy in my lap. Dane sat beside me and pulled Luke's head onto his crotch. About half of Dane's big cock was sticking out of the wide elastic band of the jockstrap. His purple fucker was drooling lube all over his furry belly.

"Eat his dick while I spank your butt," I commanded Luke, giving his ass a sharp slap for emphasis.

"No, Daddy, no!" Luke yelped like a stepped-on dog. "Don't make me! Don't make me suck his cock anymore!"

"Eat that fucking dick, you little cocksucker!" Dane angrily snarled. He forcibly shoved Luke's mouth over his jutting cockhead, and I beat his ass harder and harder. I could feel Luke's cock in my lap getting harder and harder.

Dane held Luke's pretty lips around his straining erection and forced it down his throat till Luke's neck bulged out with heavy black cock.

Thwap! Thwap! Thwap! I pummeled his quivering assflesh harder and faster till his globes shook like twin mounds of Jello. Luke winced and pumped his buttocks, grinding his dick into my groin while he noisily slobbered all over Dane's cock as if resisting eating it.

"It hurts him more if his little underpants are wet," I growled. "Piss on him, Dane."

Dane pulled Luke's head by the hair, dragging his mouth off his prick. He stood up and pulled his jockstrap down to just below his bull-balls. He had to hold his hard-on tight, and push it down so the dark, flaring head was aimed at Luke's punished buttocks.

"Please don't, man! Don't piss on me!" Luke wailed.

Dane punched out his hips and put the head of his cock right into the crack of Luke's ass. He pressed the tight white fabric of Luke's underwear up his chute. Luke squirmed and moaned.

"Hold 'im tight man—here it comes," Dane panted.

He cut loose with a jet stream of piss, filling Luke's ass-trench with his gushing yellow urine. The warm liquid ran through Luke's clenching butt-globes and soaked onto my groin. Then Dane directed his hosing spray onto my chest, and it ran in streaming rivulets till my crotch was drenched in warm, wet piss.

Dane kept on spraying. He squirted his pee up and down my "son's" writhing torso. Luke twisted his head around, and held his mouth wide open, drinking every drop.

Shlap! Shlap! Shlap! I pounded his watery ass with the flat of my hand. Piss splashed all over us, flying back onto Dane's groin.

"Now, you little cocksucker," I snarled, "eat that good black cock like you're supposed to. Show that man how you can suck a man's meat. Suck 'im!"

Dane swung his club like a ball bat, slapping Luke's face with the dreadful organ. More wet piss flew around us. Dane's big, black cock had Luke's cheeks turning an angry crimson as he flailed his face with the swinging meat. He batted a home run on Luke's flaming lips.

"Now eat it, cocksucker!" Dane ordered. "Suck my good black cock before I fuck you with it!"

Luke slurped Dane's meat into his mouth, and his red cheeks bulged with the effort. The friction from his thrusting loins was about to bring me off in my underwear.

"I'll hold 'im down, and you fuck it in 'im," I grunted.

I pulled Luke's head off Dane's meat and threw him face-down on the bed. I got his head wedged between my folded legs and Dane straddled his ass. I pulled the elastic band of my underwear below my balls, and it pushed my cock and nuts up tight against my belly.

I leaned over Luke's thrashing body to taste Dane's heavy black fucker. Dane pulled his cock and balls out of the jockstrap, and the elastic pushed the whole dark mass of his genitals into his stomach. It was just as Luke had described; the black man's root tasted spicy and funky, salty from his piss, a delectable mansmell. I sucked him till he was juicy and slimed up with spit.

"Now fuck my son," I said, drawing off and leaning back.

"No, Daddy! Please don't, Daddy!" Luke wailed. "Don't let him fuck me! Don't let him fuck your little boy!"

"Eat my cock, Son. Eat it while he fucks you," I said, dragging the front of my Jockeys down even more. I gripped my meat and ran it all over Luke's face till his features were slimy and gummed up further.

"Look what you do to me, Son. See how hard you make Daddy's cock. Feel that fucker."

"No, Daddy, that's not right. I'm your son. I'm not supposed to play with your privates."

"I can't help it. Spanking my little boy drives me wild. C'mon, make Daddy feel good. Touch it."

"No, Daddy," Luke sighed. "It ain't right. I ain't supposed to suck on my Daddy's cock. Don't make me!"

"You're gonna suck that fucking dick like I taught you, you little bastard," I growled. "Now get on it!"

Dane was holding his turgid shaft at the base and squeezing it up so that his knob swelled even more. He started pushing it against Luke's rump, teasing him with it.

"No, Daddy! He can't fuck me," Luke wailed. "I'm a boy."

"I know you're a boy. And you've got a tight little boy-ass. I'm gonna make you a fuckboy." I shoved his mouth down onto my dick and he started sucking me off.

Dane yanked Luke's underwear to one side with such force that he ripped open one leg and exposed Luke's buttocks.

"You've got to eat his asshole first," I said. I was kneading and massaging the tight muscles in Luke's back while he sucked me. "Get 'im ready for it. He's too tight if you don't."

Dane hunkered down and palmed Luke's asscheeks apart. He slurped noisily up and down Luke's dimpled, clenching buttcrack. His dark purple lips looked hot and sensual against Luke's rosy pucker as he speared his tongue inside him.

"Fuck him good," I said. "Squash that fat fucker up his little ass."

Dane's flat belly was heaving and his pecs worked with jumping muscles as he slid his root up Luke's bunghole. Dane gritted his teeth and slitted up his eyes as he ground his meat inside Luke's ass-ring. Luke groaned and moaned around my embedded cock and hunched his cute little rump. His ass dimpled and his flanks quivered as Dane drove his fuck home.

"Ah Jesus, man!" Dane gasped. "Sweet fucking ass, man. Such a sweet little boy you've got."

"Yeah! Don't he feel good inside? My sweet little son. He knows how to take a man's fuck. Work it in 'im deep. Jab his trigger till he comes!"

Dane went into the rolling undulations of a hot ass-fuck, his muscles rippling all over his sinewy, tight body. Luke was loving it and he fed more hungrily on my tool, shafting my prick through his juicy lips till I was nearly ready to cream.

Dane reached around and dragged off his jockstrap, which had been hanging around his ankles. He pulled Luke's mouth off my meat and put the jockstrap over Luke's face, the pouch covering Luke's mouth and nose, and the leg straps hanging at the sides like the reins for a horse.

"Get over here and fuck me, man," Dane commanded me. "Stick it up me hard while I fuck your son."

I crawled behind Dane and shoved my cock right into his gooey ass hole. He was as hot as fire inside. I pushed my cock all the way into his yielding assflesh and he moaned and sighed deeply. I sheathed my root all the way to the balls and pumped my cock in a quick fucking rhythm.

Dane rode Luke like a stallion, pulling backward on the reins of the strap, pulling the wet pouch across his face, dragging Luke's head back and arching his spine till Dane's grinding groin was pushed out further than his body. It was like Luke was getting a double fuck.

"Fuck that boy, man! Fuck that sweet little ass!" I panted. "Tell 'im you like it, Son. Tell 'im how you like cock up your butt."

"No, Daddy, no. It hurts!" Luke's voice was muffled from the pouch.

"C'mon, baby, feel that dick in you," I coaxed him. "Tell me it feels good. Tell Daddy you love it."

"Ah, Daddy! Oh, Daddy!" he cried.

"That's my boy, that's it. Get on it. Take his fuck, take it, boy. Deep-dick him, man!"

Suddenly, Luke splayed his legs as wide apart as they would go and frantically yelled, "Daddy! Daddy, he's gonna come in me. He's gonna shoot off inside of me!"

"Good, baby! Good! Milk 'im off like I taught you. Work that little ass of yours. Show him how Daddy's little boy makes a man's milk shoot."

I pumped harder into Dane, jabbing at his sparkplug and grinding my pubic bone against his coccyx.

"He's making me come, Daddy! I'm gonna shoot!"

"Come, baby! C'mon, Daddy's ready too."

"Ah, Daddy! Oh, Daddy! I'm coming!"

"Yeah! Yeah! Yeah!" Dane gasped.

I moaned and panted, "Here it comes, man! Take my load! Shoot off, Luke! Blow your nuts!"

Dane reached beneath Luke and pulled him into a doggie crouch. Then he began stroking him. That was all it took.

Luke creamed all over the sheets. Dane bucked and humped his juice into the deepest pit of Luke's bowels. I felt my own spewing seed gushing into Dane.

I grabbed Dane around the waist and hung on for dear life as a shattering ejaculation hit me like a baseball thrown between my legs. I shuddered throughout my body as the spasms of my jolting orgasm barreled out of my flushing nuts in hot waves. I ground my spurting knob against Dane's butt-button and felt him hosing his seed up inside of Luke.

We all three panted and gasped, moaned and groaned, grunted and strained against one another's heaving flesh till our juices were expended and we were drained. Sweat ran from our joined bodies and we collapsed in an exhausted pile on the trembling bed.

No sooner had my breathing returned to normal than my "son" piped up, "Well, that was fun. Now whatta ya wanna do?"

"We've gotta get the hell outta here," I responded.

"Y'all can spend the night if you want," Dane said, pulling his dripping black hose out of Luke's well-fucked asshole. Luke turned over on his back and his dick spat out another little dab of cream The boy was a cum factory.

There was cum all over the sheets where Luke had spit his juice out. They were wringing wet from all the piss.

"You're going to have to sleep in that by yourself," I said to Dane, pointing to it.

"It's your loss," Dane said. "I'll probably add a little to it later."

"Wish we could stick around for that," Luke said. "Every boy needs two daddies."

Stage Tricks

❖ ❖ ❖

Standing perfectly still in the blazing white light were two of the most incredibly beautiful young men I'd ever laid eyes on. . .they began moving lewdly, wriggling their asses, their loins seductively undulating. . .

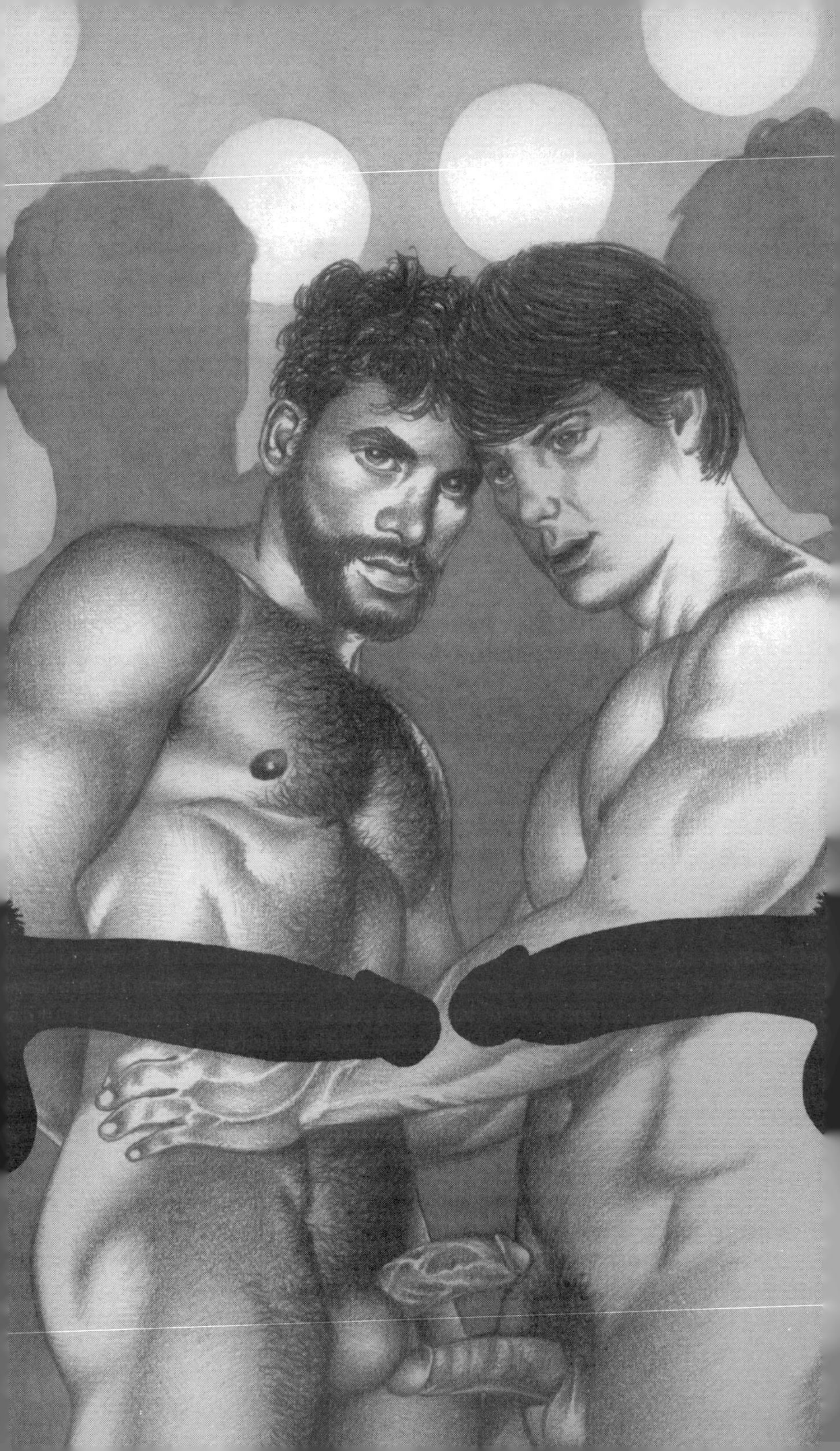

Stage Tricks

During my freshman year at college, I met a young man from Guatemala—"met" as in "fucked around with." I was studying Spanish, and Juan offered to tutor me. It's a good thing I'd already had three years of the language, given how much studying we accomplished. Juan was one of the most incredibly handsome Latin men I'd ever seen. His olive skin and high cheekbones indicated a Mayan influence, and his eyes were an arresting shade of brown with flecks of gold in them. Juan's father was a liaison to the American embassy in Guatemala City, and just before spring break, he invited me to spend a week down there. "Perfect your grammar and I promise you a good time," he said. I jumped at the chance.

I may not be able to conjugate a verb in Spanish, but I could draw a roadmap of the veins in Juan's cock from memory. And fuck? Damn—but I'm getting ahead of myself.

Anyway, the first night I arrived, Juan borrowed his brother's Jeep, and we left his house about eight o'clock. He drove us over to the Third Sector. As Juan explained it, "In Guatemala City, you have to know which Sector any numbered street is in. Like this place we're going is on Sixth Calle. But there are eight different Sixth Calles in the city, one in each Sector. And sometimes they run together and sometimes they don't, and it's confusing as hell."

We parked on a fairly crowded street under low wattage streetlamps. Juan pointed to a hanging sign in the middle of the block. It depicted a bull with a rose in its mouth. "*El Toro de la Rosa,*" he announced.

The place was packed when we got inside. It seemed to me like a pretty mixed crowd of men and women. But it was hard to see through the pall of blue smoke which drifted across the dim red lights from the ceiling. A bar stood behind three brick archways directly in the back. A stage was on our right as we entered. Four rows of folding chairs were lined up in front of it.

"This is a dingy sleaze joint," I whispered. Juan sure does know what I like.

"Yes, don't you love it?"

"Yeah."

Juan led me to the bar, a rough planked affair with broken and mismatched stools scattered in no particular order around it. The vinyl on each one was ripped and its stuffing draped out, stained and gray. Juan ordered us two beers from an overweight woman who acted bored.

"Thanks, Frenchie," he said as I paid for them. "Are Angel and Adonis on tonight?"

"Yeah," she said listlessly. "The first show's at ten."

For the first time, I noticed her Adam's apple. But her cleavage was magnificent; I didn't know how she did it. Then I began to look more closely at some of the other sultry girls sitting around. They were all guys.

The folding chairs were already beginning to fill up. The majority of the patrons in male clothing looked to be more macho and butch than I would've expected. Several of the studliest were hanging on drag queens, and there was a lot of groping going on, but no kissing. The make-up, I figured.

The lights suddenly dimmed, and Juan and I scrambled to get the last two seats on the aisle in the back row. Then the lights went completely dark and a spotlight stabbed the bare stage with a piercing beam.

A voice boomed out from hidden loudspeakers, dragging out every syllable. "Ladies and gentlemen," then pausing for dramatic effect, "Pee!"

Blaring music crashed from all around us, a throbbing, insistent drum-roll that crested to an ear-splitting crescendo. I expected everybody to get up and start pissing to that barked announcement.

A stunning blond drag queen strode majestically onto the stage and into the spotlight.

"That's Pee," Juan whispered.

"A fucking drag show," I thought, irritatedly. Definitely not my idea of a good time.

The music chopped off the instant Pee stopped center stage. Her Oriental gown, lavishly decorated with gold and silver leaves, dragons and flowers in abundance, flowed gracefully to her shapely ankles. She stared at everyone in the audience, her eyes sweeping the room slowly. The bar grew deathly quiet.

The tinkle of a music-box wafted from the speakers in tiny, hesitant notes. Pee put her hand to one ear, listening intently. Her other hand floated in the air like a soaring butterfly. The music swelled, an Asian melody which hauntingly rose and dipped in subtle waves. Palms together as though praying, her folded arms perfectly horizontal, Pee began a graceful, swaying dance. I was not prepared for its elegant and fluid, near classical execution.

As she concluded her performance, I found myself standing along with the crowd and applauding, though I didn't exactly find all this real exciting. But then, from where we sat, I saw a young man locking the front door. The lights went so dim I could barely see. I sensed a collective holding of breath.

A man's disembodied voice rang out: "And now ladies and gentlemen, *El Toro de la Rosa* is proud to present, from Mexico City, our featured entertainers for the evening." He paused and the music soared dramatically. "The incomparable talents of—Angel and Adonis!"

A searing spotlight shot onto the stage, and applause erupted simultaneously.

Now this was more like it! Standing perfectly still in the blazing white light were two of the most incredibly beautiful young men I'd ever laid eyes on. They were wearing only very skimpy loincloths. One of the performers was a warm brown cocoa color; the other was a striking blond youth with skin like bronze. Their muscled and perfectly proportioned torsos were completely hairless, gleaming with oil which glistened in the spotlight.

"Adonis is the black guy. Angel is the blond," Juan whispered in my ear.

A large, padded platform had been moved onto the stage while it was dark and they stood in front of it. I could barely make out a live drummer seated to the left of the stage. He set up a slow cadence on the kettle drum, very deep and bass. Their striated arms moved sinuously up and down in time with the measured beats.

Then they turned sideways and stared intently into one another's eyes. Their hips moved suggestively in unison, slowly at first then more rapidly as the drum increased its tempo. A rapid thrumming on the snare drum and they began moving lewdly, wriggling their asses, their loins seductively undulating. With exquisite, erotic grace, they danced before one another, never touching, staring, staring, staring. They ignored their audience, as if the two of them were alone.

Their magnificent bodies were soon sheened with sweat and they fairly glowed as they danced a perfectly choreographed dance of love. You could tell it was that. They swayed sensuously before each other, teasing, tantalizing, moving their bodies in time with the lustful drum. It was beautiful.

Then their faces clouded. They backed away from each other, each moving to opposite ends of the stage. They turned their backs on each other and you could tell there was a problem in their relationship. They stayed rigidly still for a moment. Then the drum banged heavily, again and again: Boom! Boom! Boom!

The two boys turned and raced toward the platform in the center. Five feet from it, they bounded into the air at the same instant. Somersaulting, they landed on the padded surface facing one another. Then it got hot.

Tentatively, each touched the other's chest with his fingertips, stroking and trailing languidly over hard, smooth skin. The platform was so elevated that we could see that the performers were naked under their loincloths. We could see them getting hard. The beat of the drums became more intense. Their palms glided more swiftly over their bodies. They got harder. The material began to tent.

I got harder. The loincloths lifted as their cocks swelled from beneath the draped fabric. They felt each other, lifting their balls and stroking their penises. Slowly, they stripped each other. They stood and their faces shone with an eager glee.

They both had prodigiously out-sized equipment, tomato-sized balls swinging beneath fully erect and immense cocks, longer than I'd ever seen. Their pubic hair had been shaved and their flat groins and bellies accentuated the monstrous length of their cocks. I found their naked crotches exciting. Their pubic areas were as smooth and slick as their gleaming asses.

I felt Juan's hand on my leg, stroking between my thighs. I put my hand in his lap. He was hard, and I caressed the swollen lump in his crotch. Not speaking, but staring fixedly at the boys, we groped each other. Around us, I sensed others doing the same. There was a rustle of clothing, and the sounds of zippers singing open, pants being pushed down, and heavy breathing.

The boys were now grinding their naked crotches together, arms behind them, flanks punched out and only their genitals touching. They worked their stiff dicks up under each other's balls and lifted them. They took turns grinding their cocks between each other's legs and lewdly moving them in and out. Their dicks were so big, we could see their heads protruding from their backsides, first one, then the other as they hip-fucked each other.

Juan unzipped my fly and snaked his hand inside. His fingers felt hot as he slipped them into my underwear. Impatiently, I dug out his prick, the fat wedge of his hard-on lubing over my fingers. I masturbated him slowly. The blond Angel knelt reverently before Adonis's cock. He suckled on his partner's balls.

Juan dragged my cock out of my pants, and I snapped them open and pushed them down to my knees. Angel stuck his tongue out all the way and washed the dark youth's cock until the chocolate shank gleamed with spit. Adonis leaned backward, arching his spine till he was bent double, his palms flat on the platform. His cock was immense and Angel worshiped on it with all his mouth.

I pushed my jeans to my ankles, spread my legs, and Juan went down on me. His soft wet lips sheathed my dong, and I scooted my butt to the edge of the seat. Juan lip-stroked my cock until I was about ready to come. I pulled his head off and went down on him. Around me, I heard other men doing the same. Juan tasted delicious. I was beginning to love the taste of his meat. I worked the bloated shaft down my throat and felt him throbbing hard inside me until he frantically dragged my head off his cock.

"Not yet. Get naked," he whispered huskily.

On the stage, Adonis was fucking Angel. They were standing upright, just the black cock pumping in and out of the blond's asshole. The dark boy's rump flexed and dimpled as he slowly pistoned his meat to Angel while he squeezed on his tits.

❖

Angel stroked his cock in a slow, languid way, an expression of ecstasy on his face, head thrown back with his eyes closed and resting on Adonis's shoulder. Again, it was as if they were all alone on the lighted stage, unaware of the audience, half of whom were now naked and sucking and fucking one another. The smell of sex was thick in the smoky air.

I felt someone standing beside me. In the reflected light from the stage, I saw he was naked. And all man.

The dark giant had a magnificent torso, gleaming like a lustrous plum in the light, with deep muscles reflecting shadows over his statuesque frame. He was so tall, his cock was above my head and swinging like a construction boom. The fucking thing was mammoth.

I became aware of Juan at my side, stripping. Other men around us were doing the same. I stood, and the black guy raised my head to his and drove the largest tongue I'd ever felt down my throat. It felt as big as Juan's cock. He pulled it out of my mouth, bent over, and put his large purple lips to my ear.

"You can call me Carlos," he whispered, tonguing the words in.

Carlos turned me around and bent me over, squatted down, and started licking on my hole. I found Juan's cock in my face and I sucked his meat while I cut my eyes to the stage. Angel and Adonis were really fucking now. Sweat poured off their heated bodies in virtual rivers, glistening in the spotlight. Angel had gone to all fours and Adonis was slamming into him with his legs slightly bent, his palms flat on Angel's back, ass-grinding his cock in a fury.

Each time Adonis pulled out his cock, we could see the thick veins on his driving meat. Then he jacked Angel off beneath his belly, hanging onto his back and buttfucking him like a dog, his black meat spearing into the hole so fast, it became a driving blur. Men panted and gasped and wheezed all around us. I sucked harder on Juan.

Carlos' huge tongue up my butt felt like a giant cock, spiking in and out of my guts. Then I felt someone crawl under my bent-over form. Whoever it was started sucking on my dick. I felt my nuts ready to blow. The drum was pounding an incessant Caribbean rhythm, the closest thing I've heard to a fuck put to music.

Carlos pulled his tongue out of my asshole. His sweaty, naked body slithered up my back and I was afraid he wanted to fuck me. There was no way I could handle a joint that big, but he grabbed me around the chest instead, and slid his meat between my legs.

He reached under me to where the guy was blowing me and

pushed my balls up into their sockets. I would've thought that would hurt, but it didn't. Juan had moved off to the side a little so the guy could suck me better and I was still mouthing his rod for all I was worth. Carlos fucked his log between my legs till the knob was nudging at my sucker's chin. I reached down to my groin area and got a handful of slobbery lips and squashed dick.

"I like to get off this way," Carlos panted in my ear, biting it. "Between your legs. Squeeze 'em tight." I did, and he rutted in and out in a frenzy.

On the stage, Adonis was ready to blow. He pulled his cock out of Angel and Angel immediately rolled onto his back. Adonis stood straddling him with his long legs, still sideways to us, furiously pumping his cock. Angel started whipping on his big fucktool.

"Come on me! Come on me!" he yelled.

"Come! Come! Come!" Adonis gasped through gnashed teeth and a grimace of orgasm on his face. They loudly groaned and moaned, grunting piggishly and the drumming ceased abruptly.

For the first time, they turned only their heads to the crowd and shouted in unison, "Come! Come! Come!"

And then, good God, they unloaded their jizz! I never saw anything like it. Great spewing fountains of their spunk ripped out simultaneously, Adonis literally hosing down Angel's writhing torso with huge gushers of cream. Angel's milk shot straight up in the air for a good five feet, arching in the spotlight like a spurting garden hose. His streaming jism spewed all the way to Adonis's face where it dripped down his dark body. It was the most beautiful sight I'd ever seen, rivers of white on his chocolate skin!

Guys all around us were going off at the same time. My nuts started flushing jizz. I shot my load in the feeding guy's mouth and Juan pumped his juice to me. I reached between my legs and felt Carlos's pole as he shot off on my sucker's chest, another creamy river that I smeared around with my hands. The man sucking me jacked off all over my feet. My body was wracked with anguished lust and I sagged against Juan in exhaustion. Juan held me tightly in his big strong arms as I shuddered out the last of my load.

It was at that moment that the front door shattered open and about a dozen cops flooded in.

All hell broke loose. Powerful flashlights stabbed all over the room like a crazed kaleidoscope. Men shouted and screamed. The cops started herding people in groups. Chaos broke out in the front rows as men scrambled to dress and flee. I barely had time to realize what was going on.

But suddenly, Juan and I were separated. I was terrified.

In the pandemonium, Carlos dragged me backward and half-carried me through a curtained doorway off to one side of the bar. "Follow me!" he hissed and we ran down a long hall. I heard footsteps behind us. We rounded a corner at breakneck speed and raced across a courtyard. My balls flopped and ached as we flew up a flight of wooden stairs.

At the first landing, I jerked my head back and looked down into the courtyard. I was relieved to see Juan and a little naked guy following us. Carlos ran down the gallery and fumbled with the lock of a door. He threw it open and we rushed in, Juan and the little fellow right behind.

"This is my apartment," Carlos said. He locked the door and peeked through a curtain. I joined him. "Shh," he whispered.

We listened and heard nothing. The courtyard remained empty.

"That was a close call," the short kid standing beside Juan said.

Carlos introduced us. "This is Antonio, but everybody calls him Tony."

"You look as good as you taste, boy," Tony said with a wicked grin. "That was some load you fed me."

So this had been my little sucker. Incongruously, we shook hands. He was cute.

"What was that shit all about?" I asked the room in general.

Tony said, "Aw, they pull that crap every once in awhile—gets their hormones going. They're a bunch of fucking sadists."

"Most of them probably came in their pants tonight," Carlos said.

"Speaking of coming," I said. "That Adonis and Angel are something, huh?"

"Looks good, doesn't it?" Tony asked.

"That's an understatement."

"You oughtta see the midnight show."

"They do it again, come like that?" I asked, disbelievingly.

"Sixty cc syringes on the backside of their dicks for the special effects," Tony said with a smirk.

"And turkey basters for the grand finale," Carlos said with a chuckle.

"They mix up heavy cream with whipping cream," confessed Tony. "But it looks great in the light, huh?"

I'd just as soon not known about the stage tricks. But when the four of us came later, there was no mistaking the real thing. Turkey basters, indeed!

EQUAL OPPORTUNITY

❖ ❖ ❖

He sheathed his pink, cut head inside my dickflesh and it felt like we were joined that way. Docking, he called it, a good word for what our knobs were doing to one another inside the undulating blanket of dark black skin. . .

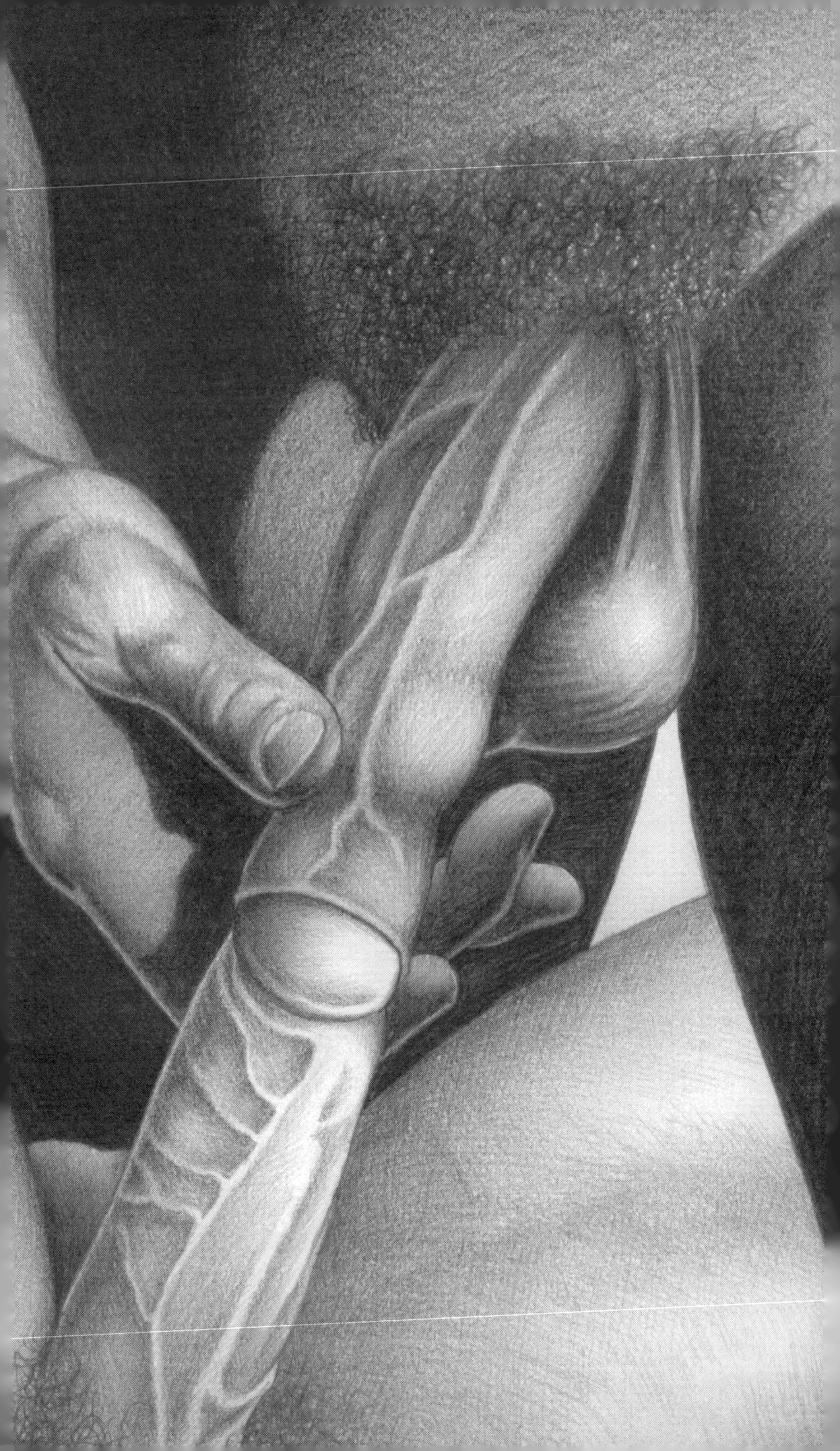

EQUAL OPPORTUNITY

"We've got a plethora of problems here."

"Plethora?"

"Means we're up to our asses in them."

I was having a discussion with my new hired helper about the severe destruction we had experienced from a big storm on the golf course. Some of the greens had been under water for practically three days and the turf would suffer for that. The sand traps looked like no man's land from the erosion that had washed all the soil to a flat pit in the center. A huge old tree had been split by lightning and would have to be removed from where it lay on its side. I didn't care a fig for golf myself, but the contract with the country club was the most profitable of my maintenance accounts. I think they awarded it to me to make themselves more politically correct. I call my company 4L Service, from my motto: Louie's Lawns Live Long. Kind of corny; but people seem to remember it.

The Seventies were a time of rising consciousness, and the board members were in the midst of a battle with the city over their admissions policy, so they could point to me as an example of minority hiring. But there was no way my black ass would ever be considered for acceptance. Not that I would want to associate with those types.

I had hired little blond Randy with some of the same considerations in mind. My other ten employees were black. Besides, he dressed up a work crew more than you could believe. I had a couple of older white customers, in their middle thirties like me, whom I'd met in the gay bar we frequented, who said he was the prettiest little thing to come down the pike. Unfortunately, he was straight. Or so I'd been told by a guy I know in the pool business who had recommended him.

I set my men to raking the sand traps and mowing the grass while Randy and I tackled the fallen tree that blocked the back entrance of the club house. After a couple of hours hacking at branches with our hatchets, Randy said he had to use the bathroom.

"Piss over in those bushes," I said. "Nobody can see you." I pointed across the green about five hundred yards away.

"Not that, Louie," Randy piped. "Do I have to spell it out for you?"

If he'd been any of my other men, I'd have told him to go farther back into the trees that surrounded the golf course. That may sound racist, but there were no facilities at this club for the hired help, and I really didn't want my men embarrassed by any of the more intolerant members of the restricted country club. And besides, I knew the bathrooms were just inside the rear door which we'd finally gotten unblocked. So I told Randy to go in there.

After twenty minutes had passed, I began to get suspicious about what was taking him so long. So without thinking too much about it, I sauntered off to find him. The bathrooms are in a tiled passageway which leads to the locker rooms and showers, as I noticed by the signs. Randy wasn't in the bathroom. This was the only exit without entering the building proper, and I couldn't imagine where he'd gone.

Not hearing any evidence that it was occupied, I slipped down the hall to the men's locker room. I listened to the silence at the door before pushing it open and sneaking in. No showers were running. There was a bench running down the center of the room, with lockers on both sides of it. I saw Randy's jeans and red tee shirt wadded up on the other end, his tennis shoes on the floor beneath them.

What the fuck was he doing? I crept toward a redwood structure which I figured was a sauna. Turned out, it was a steam room. One glass window faced the side away from me. At the door, I listened again. Then I inched my head around the corner so I could peer into the steamy room. I thought my eyes would pop out.

In the dim light, and through crystal droplets fogging the glass, I could see Randy leaning against one wall. He was naked, and an older guy was sucking his cock, the white hair on his head a rapid blur. Randy was slumped back, his hips thrust out and face-fucking the guy, feeding him dick with his hands on each side of the man's bobbing head. I started boning up.

As my eyes adjusted to the dimness, I saw the guy wasn't all that bad, even though he did have a double chin. He'd cup Randy's balls and pull them to just beneath the lower one, taking all the good-sized cock the boy had. Then he'd pull off till just the head was lodged inside his mouth, looking up at Randy and mouthing the knob. I could see his tongue really working the kid over. And the older dude certainly had a hefty hunk of sausage pumping between his spread-open legs. He was jacking himself harder and faster, gyrating his pelvis in time with his sucking. Hot as hell to watch.

Suddenly, Randy's head swiveled and his eyes locked onto mine. My forehead was pressed up against the glass. He looked at me with lust-drugged eyes. Then he licked his moist lips and, with a jerk of his head, motioned for me to come in. The man continued sucking as I slipped inside the door. Randy edged away from the wall and the man kneed after him. I wedged in behind Randy and touched his sweating body. He slumped back against me. The man didn't miss a stroke on Randy's cock as he gazed up at my face over Randy's shoulder.

"Hold me tight," Randy whispered in my ear.

It was weird for me—to be so turned on, just clutching Randy's bare, slick body against my fully clothed one. That seemed to be what he wanted, just to be held fast while the guy gave him head. I didn't even take out my cock, but ground my pelvis against Randy's naked and quivering ass globes. I caressed his smooth, hairless chest and twisted his nipples. He was going to have hickeys for weeks on his slender neck as he leaned back into my embrace and I fed hungrily in the little hollows at his shoulders. Then he turned his face and I tongue-fucked his pretty mouth. He sucked hungrily on my mouth-meat, and I curled it at the tip and gave his throat a rattlesnake wiggle.

I reached down to Randy's balls and fed his dick to the man, pulling Randy's concave belly against me. Randy groaned and started grunting. His chest was heaving like an accordion bellows. His buttocks were pumping harder and faster against my groin. I rutted into the friction.

Randy bit his lower lip, squeezed his eyes shut, and pumped his flanks even faster. We came up for air and he threw back his head and rolled it around on my shoulder, his plastered wet hair scraping my cheek. He was coming. I could see the man swallowing his load. The sight nearly made me shoot off in my pants. My own cock was painfully hard and snaking out of my underwear. I gripped myself, pushed the fat head all the way out of the leg band of my briefs and ground my cock against Randy's rump and through the khaki material of my pants.

I got a good friction going on the shaft and rubbed my cockhead vigorously between his butt cheeks. In seconds, my cock started shooting inside my drawers. I felt the gushers flowing out, the tenseness in my groin let fly. I sagged against the wall, dragging Randy backward as my juice bolted out in my pants. There was so much cum that a milky patch began to spread across my crotch, the wetness making them darker, and slimier on his butt.

I released Randy with a light kiss and then backed out of the room, pushing the door open with my butt and trying for some fresh air after inhaling so much steam. And then thought I would die as I heard a gravelly voice harshly demand, "What the hell are you doing in here?"

I shot my face back over my shoulder and saw a paunchy, middle-aged fellow in pastel blue shorts and a bright yellow golf shirt staring at me as if I were from another planet. The expression on his face suggested he was seeing a hunk of rotten liver before him. I swiftly turned to face him, and when he got a gander at my swollen dick with the spreading patch of cum, his eyes really did pop out. He looked like that comedian that gets no respect.

"I asked you a question, boy!" he hissed. He really said that.

"I ain't your fucking boy!" I retorted just as vehemently.

He stood there with his lips pursed together so tightly, he looked like he had terminal constipation. His face was livid, a beef-and-bourbon red. Then the door from the steam room opened. Randy and the man walked out. Naked. I couldn't help but look at Randy's dick, now wilting, but still on a semi. The older man's dick was coated with the white stuff. A little late cum dripped off the head. My man saw it.

"Oh Jesus!" he gasped. "Queers and niggers!" And he ran out of there as if he'd been shot in the ass with a BB gun.

There was a guilty look on Randy's young face as he stared at me. The older man with Randy wore a contented mask. He opened his locker and calmly began dressing. There was a feverish expression in my eyes as I looked at Randy.

"We'd better get out of here," I said. "Hurry up, Randy, get dressed."

The older man turned around and looked at me kind of funny, but he didn't say anything immediately. Randy skinned into his jeans, stuck his tee shirt down the back of his pants.

"This is Leonard," Randy said when we were once more what society calls "decent." Leonard had a firm handshake, actually warm.

"I can just imagine what stories old Max is telling in the bar," said Leonard. "Asshole's the only one that didn't know I'm the dirty little secret in the bathroom the members don't tell their sainted wives about. Hope to see you guys around." With that, he left and Randy and I returned to our job.

"Thought you were straight," I said peevishly as Randy and I went back to work, now sawing the main trunk of the tree with a two-man blade.

"I thought *you* were straight, Louie," he said, pushing the two-handled saw more forcefully, like jabbing it at me.

I shoved it right back at him. "And with that old geezer!"

"Old guys know how to suck cock," he said impishly. "You got a problem with that?" Saw.

"No. How'd he come onto you?" Saw.

"In the bathroom, while I was in the stall. Reached his hand under the partition." Saw.

"Why not let him get you off in there? Why strip down and do it in the steam room?" Pushing the blade hard.

"He said it was more private. And he wanted to see me naked." Vengefully returned.

"On my time." A really long and swift stroke.

"Yeah, Louie. You jealous?" The same thing back.

"Might be a little of that," I said, giving him a particularly hard shove.

"Your cock was sure hard enough. I felt that. And you came in your pants, huh?" Shoving back with equal force.

"Yeah—well." I took the swing and let him drag it back.

"Some kind of private." Harder sawing.

"You mind I fucked with you?" I asked, keeping up with his swifter rhythm.

"I've been wantin' you to. Afraid you'd fire me if you found out." Stroke.

"I'm sure as hell not going to fire you." Saw.

"What are you going to do?" Saw.

"Well, since you're so generous—" Nearing the bottom of the tree and now the saw is truly singing.

"I want you to fuck me, Louie." And the tree split down the middle with a loud crack.

Leaning back and gripping my spine, I stretched and said, "That might be considered sexual harassment."

"It will be sexual harassment if you don't," Randy said with a positively wicked glint in his blue eyes, staring at my cum-soaked crotch.

"In that case, I guess I'd better."

Randy and I loaded up the larger of the two trucks, and I directed the rest of the crew to finish up. "Then knock off, since I won't be coming back today."

On the ride over to my apartment, Randy kept his hand on my leg the whole time, when he wasn't digging his hand down my pants and sliming around in the sticky goo. He sucked on my neck with that little mouth just made for sex. Ducking down on the seat while we were in the midst of traffic, Randy unzipped my fly. Then he glommed his mouth on the gap and tongued the stiff shaft of my prick inside my pants.

He fumbled my cock all the way out, then made love to my jutting organ beneath the steering wheel. My legs quivered and my foot pressed unsteadily on the accelerator. He never sucked me all the way in, but contented himself with low moans and sighs as he rubbed his cheeks and face with the swollen knob, licking my pre-cum as if it was the sweetest nectar. At a traffic light, he dug out my balls and slobbered them up till I thought I was going to shoot.

By the time we'd gotten into the bedroom, I was ready to blow my nuts again.

Randy's body was smooth and lithe, melding into my arms as I stripped him naked. His skin was satiny and sheened to a burnished copper, except for a narrow V at his groin where his pubic bush grew a luxuriant golden. He kissed with me and his lips were firm and yielding, sweet tasting and young. His dick wasn't huge but hard as flesh-wrapped steel, and he pushed it into my groin.

"Keep your underwear on," Randy said as I started stripping out of my clothes. "I love looking at white underwear on a black guy's skin."

I left my Jockeys on, glided onto the bed, and flopped to my back. I dragged Randy's compliant body on top of me. My boner was lodged up in the V of my groin and extended to my hips. Randy's naked loins pushed against me hard, undulating and thrusting against my pelvis. My briefs were still wet, and the lubrication of my cum made it feel hot as hell. I mouthed his face before seeking the deep-tongued kiss. Randy sucked my tongue. We dueled, out and in, over and under, around our teeth. Randy drove his slender tongue like a feeding minnow between my lips and teeth, all around my mouth and pressing against the insides of my gums. Nothing inexperienced about this kid; I could tell he'd been scraping his carrot in other places.

Randy's ass-globes were smooth and taut with youthful muscles. I kneaded and caressed his cheeks, feeling him tense and relax, flex and coil.

Randy slid down between my legs, rolled my damp underwear to my thighs, and gobbled on my uncut dick like he was starving, slurping and dick-licking on my root so loudly, it sounded like an animal's feeding. I loved getting my cock sucked like that, but a pulsing sensation in my balls told me I was in danger of shooting off right then.

I pulled Randy up from his feeding frenzy, and he held our black and white dicks together, tightly around the middle and squeezing up the shafts so the heads swelled into our crotches. By dragging my foreskin off the bone, he sheathed his pink, cut head inside my dickflesh and it felt like we were joined that way. Docking, he called it, a good word for what our knobs were doing to one another inside the undulating blanket of dark black skin. Lube drool poured out of both of us, and the slime created delirious sensations of dick-fucking between us. My piss-slit was so sensitive I could feel his cum-hole jabbing against it, like a tiny round mouth. Again, I was close to coming. Too close.

I scrambled backward and turned him onto his belly. "Let me get you ready," I whispered in his ear as I sank to my knees behind him. I spread Randy's delicious little cheeks apart with both palms and went to work on his hole, licking his sweet flesh in concentric circles till I zeroed in and skewered right up into his puckered ring. I tongue-fucked his bittersweet asshole till he was slimed up and slobbered enough to fuck.

Eating ass makes me lube a lot, and my cock was literally dripping to get inside him. I flopped him over again, lifted his legs in the air, and slid wetly up his sweaty backside till my knob was pressing into his tight pucker. But I wanted to savor every patch of him, so I pulled his cock back like a pistol trigger and went down on his hard, young root. His cockskin was smooth, ripe, hot, luscious, and bursting with seed.

He pulled me off. "I'm too close," he panted.

Randy arched his spine, reached behind him and spread his ass for me. I pushed the head of my cock against his slobbery hole. We both gasped as I slowly eased my stiff cock up Randy's clenching buttocks, hunching my way deeper and deeper.

Randy's butthole was the tightest furnace I'd ever gotten my dick into. His milking muscles rippled up and down my shaft, threatening to bring me off any second. My fist, working on his fat, red knob was all gooey and webbed with sticky lube which kept streaming out of his bulbous head.

I pushed my cock into him all the way. Then he went completely crazy, thrashing and moaning, trembling and shivering all over like he was having a fit. I held him tightly to me and stroked his sweating body, hunching in deeper all the while. He kept grunting and sighing as I worked more meat up his tight chute. I knew I had him when he relaxed and started breathing deeply. Then he came. He tensed up, then shivered, and his juice spat out like a fucking faucet.

"Don't stop, Louis! I'm gonna go again!"

"You mean you're gonna come again?"

"Yeah! Yes! Fuck me!"

So I did. I had to hold back from coming myself when I saw him shooting all over again. But I dragged his face sideways to me. Then I started kissing him and sucking his tongue till it stuck out of his mouth like a dick while I worked my cock in his hole for as long as I could hold out. That wasn't very long, he was so hot inside.

I went into the slow, rolling motions of steady hard-dicking, content in that moment of bliss. Randy sure knew how to take a guy's fuck. He pushed his young, round ass up in the air, and I drove my pile driver in and out of his vise-like hole.

I went into a ramming, spiking man-fuck and drilled Randy's perfect butt with deep, hard pumping thrusts. He writhed and trembled beneath the force of my deep-dicking strokes. I straight-armed up on his little round butt and ground frenziedly into his bowels. My loins pounded my slapping balls noisily against his rump and we sweated and grunted at our furious fuck.

"Ah shit! Oh fuck! Oh God! I'm gonna come!" Randy panted.

"Blow your nuts, kid! Shoot it, baby!" I yelled.

"Yeah! Yeah! Yeah!" he cried.

I shot off then. Waves of spasmodic ecstasy washed over me, and I ejaculated with all the fury of an explosion blasting off between my legs. In streaming rivers, my creaming cock spewed out more dick-gravy than I ever remembered as my guts wrenched out my prick-spit.

I clutched Randy's throbbing crank in my hand, fisted him off, and felt his spunk begin to explode. His spurting milk webbed my fingers and I jerked him off onto his belly, his second shot equaling the first in its intensity.

His torso flailed like a wild thing as he madly shot off his third load. He had that thin, milky cum that shoots like an open hydrant, and it spat all the way to his hair. We shuddered to a convulsive climax. I fell beside him and cradled his head to my neck, kissing his damp golden hair.

"Remember what that old guy at the club yelled?" he said, timidly all of a sudden.

"Yeah, don't remind me."

"Seems like we've got a lot in common, huh?"

"Yeah, c'mere." And I kissed him again.

During the next two weeks I became addicted to Randy's little ass, and my wiener got to know his sweet buns like a second home. That organ in my chest got heavily involved as well. I had him working with me as we raked the sand traps one afternoon. As I leaned back to stretch my aching muscles, I saw Leonard, the initial cause of our coming together so to speak, approaching from the greens in a golf cart. Randy waved and they greeted one another like nodding acquaintances as Leonard jerked to a stop beside us and stepped out.

He walked up to me rather hesitantly. "Can we talk a minute, Louie?" he asked. "In private."

"I guess," I said, feeling somehow like he was threatening me. We walked to an oak tree and entered the cooler shade before he said anything else.

"I don't quite know how to say this," he faltered. "I've thought of it over and over while I was tossing and turning all night. So I'll just come out and tell you the truth. We need you."

"How you mean, need?" I asked, cocking my head to one side.

"The city's gonna pull our license to operate unless we integrate," he said, sort of like he was dumping it off his mind. "I'm not proud of having to tell you this. It makes me feel like shit, if you wanna know the truth. I've been bucking the chairman of the admissions committee for years to open up, told them it would come to this. Now they've got no choice, admit blacks and Jews, or shut down. These fancy folks don't relish giving up their club, so they're backed into a corner. You realize you'd be a token for a little while, no getting around it. But folks here know you, have seen you around the place for years, know you're always friendly and polite. Besides that, you're a businessman. It would be good for you, so...how about it?" Leonard finished his little set speech and stood there expectantly.

There was defiance in my voice when I at last ended the pregnant silence. "I don't go places I'm not welcome, or comfortable in. 'Fraid you've got the wrong guy."

"Goddammit, Louie," he sputtered. "They already voted you in. For an annual fee of ten dollars."

"Not interested." In truth, I was becoming highly insulted. I made enough money to pay the regular dues.

"Please, Louie," Leonard asked. "Give it a try. You might like it, the pool and all, the restaurant."

"I'm sure old 'queers-and-niggers' that caught us in the bathroom would be amused, me swimming next to him," I said, with just a tiny touch of glee at the thought.

"That's the best part of it—what I was saving for last."

"What's that?"

"That's Max, the chairman of admissions. He was out with the gout when we voted. He'll be hearing about it for the first time when we introduce you as the new member." And here his smile used up all his double chins.

I clapped my hand on his shoulder, and we both went into a laughing fit. When we got through hanging onto each other, I asked, "What about Randy? Can he use the pool?"

"We'll tell 'em he's your son," Leonard said, nearly choking, wiping his eyes with a handkerchief. "I'm sure old Max won't stick around very long."

Well, to make a long story short, the pool is relaxing and Randy loves it, though I still hate golf.

RUBE AWAKENING

❖ ❖ ❖

There in the dark and hot prison cell, this huge, bald black man started breathing new life into me. His long, black bone was completely wedged in my crack, and he began gently gliding it through the wetness.

Rube Awakening

Looking back on it now, I can see I had to be the dumbest hick that ever came off the mountain. I was a cow-licked, blond burr-head with a big old dopey grin and blue eyes—a good-natured guy, in spite of my background. My folks belonged to this tiny sect of people who handle snakes during the Sunday services. This is supposed to show their faith in overpowering the devil, symbolized by the snake. A lot of them got bitten, and I did too, though in a different way. There were about forty people in our congregation, and they came from miles around our neck of the woods up in the mountains of Tennessee. What little I knew of the world came from a neighbor's television, although us eight kids were not allowed to see one.

At eighteen, I was next to the oldest, my brother having lit out for greener pastures the year before. You might say I had a crisis of faith when the snake in my pants had to be wrestled with more than the devil. That crisis reached epic proportions when I started getting sexed up watching my daddy's brood sow getting fucked. The stud hog's cock turned me on. I didn't think there were too many other virgins my age, but I knew for sure that I was one.

I didn't say a word to anybody the morning I took off, imitating my older brother. I had fourteen dollars and forty cents to my name, a pair of coveralls, work boots, and no shirt. I made my way down to the two-lane blacktop that ran about a mile from our house, stuck out my thumb, and by the next day, I was in Chattanooga. To make a long story short.

My education began almost right away. I had only slept spottily during the night in a guy's pickup truck, and he'd dropped me off in town just as the sun was rising. I had to piss in the worst possible way. So I found a public bathroom in a park at the center of town. Two guys were standing next to each other in front of the wall toilets when I went in and they sort of jumped apart at the sound of my footsteps. I didn't pay much attention to them, but went back toward a row of stalls.

They didn't have any doors on them and I was embarrassed. I know how dumb that sounds, but I really was. In our house, the bathroom door had a lock on it, and it was a sin to see somebody naked. Nevertheless, I dropped the front of my coveralls, hauled out my big, long devil and hosed off a good horsecock piss. Felt almost as good as coming, though the only experience I'd had with that was palm-loading.

Then somebody entered the stall next to mine. That was the first time I became aware of a hole cut in the wooden partition. Well, just about the same time that the guy sat down on the toilet, my damned coveralls fell down, exposing my ass and all my considerable equipment. I never wore drawers anyway, and I blushed all over when I saw his eye looking through the hole at me. I guess me stripping like that, the minute he entered, gave him courage.

"Stick it through," he whispered immediately.

Well, I wasn't *that* dumb. *"It"* could only mean one thing. And my big devil knew it before I did. My cock started swelling in my fist, and the man brought his mouth to the hole and licked all around his lips. Trembling and shaking all over, I turned to the wall with my twisted coveralls around my ankles, stuck my cock through the hole and into his mouth. He couldn't have gotten more than three or four lip strokes on that whanger before the devil started spitting his juice. And I thought I was going to fall over backward from the jolt that shuddered through my groin. I held onto the top of the partition, lifted my feet off the floor, squeezed my eyes shut tight, and trembled and shook so hard, the damned thing rattled and started to bend.

And my legs almost collapsed as I dropped back down, sucked and drained dry before I knew what had hit me. I didn't realize what a chance I'd taken, till I recovered myself sufficiently to look around.

There were two guys standing at the open stall door, with their hard dicks out and jacking, watching me and smiling.

"Good show, boy," one of them said. "Can I have a taste?"

I just stood there, struck dumb. Then the man who'd asked the question pulled a ten dollar bill out the side of his pocket just enough for me to see the number. Confused and wide-eyed, I swallowed hard and shook my head. Then without saying a word, I hauled up my coveralls and fairly ran out of there.

Talk about a religious experience! Nothing in my life had ever left such a profound impression on me. I know it's difficult to believe that anyone could be so sheltered in this day and age, but nothing before had prepared me for the enormity of that first time a man's mouth sank down on my root.

I didn't stray too far from the park after that. And I won't bore you overmuch about what I was thinking on. Just that it seemed to me that the good Lord knew what He was doing when He made our bodies like His, and there wasn't much point in folks looking for the devil all the time. And anything that He created, anything that felt that damned good, couldn't be wrong at all.

There was a diner across the street, and I went in there and got a seat by the window where I could look out at the bathrooms. While I was having a fine breakfast, I studied the comings and goings across the way. There were a couple of men in suits, a boy on a bicycle, a man who took off his wedding ring before he went in, and a farmer in a pickup truck. Then two black kids went in together and came out with satisfied grins. By the time I'd finished my coffee, I was stiff again.

By adjusting my boner straight up to my belly, I was able to get out of the booth and pay for my meal. My leg was wet from lube-juice seeping out of my cockhead. When I got back to the bathroom, I was as hard as a log. This time, there were three men at the urinals standing next to one another. They turned their heads at my approach. One of them was the guy who'd asked could he have a taste of my meat, and he smiled when he saw me. I gave him my distinctive big old dopey grin. (Thing is, I knew it looked good on me.) He was on the end and he motioned me to stand next to him. I forgot all about my earlier shyness.

As I took up my place in the line, I saw that all the men were jacking their hard-ons, and their dicks were wet, like they'd been sucking on them. I unsnapped one side of my coveralls and wrestled Old Devil out through the gap. He was really leaking now, pre-cum practically running out of my skin-nozzle. They all stared, and the man next to me bent over and started licking the seepage off my prod. Then he skinned back my cockhead and sucked my shank down his throat. He was even better at it than the first. Then the man next to him backed off and the third stranger squatted and went down on his meat. He had a God-awful hunk of it, too.

My sucker clutched my asscheeks in his hands and guided me over beside the man getting sucked. That man reached down and got my hand and pulled it over to his cock. It was hot as hell, feeling him getting sucked off, all juicy and wet with slobber as the other man fed on his meat. I played with his balls while he was getting sucked, and he fed my cock to the bobbing face at my groin.

When I heard the man grunting real hard, I felt his nuts contract. "I'm coming!" he gasped through clenched teeth. He started moving his hips and face-fucking so fast, I forgot about my dick and held the man's head. I watched the man on his rod go pig-crazy as he started blowing off. His neck was working like a turkey gobbler's as he sucked off that man's load of jism.

When I saw the cum running out the sides of the sucker's mouth, that jolted the juice out of Old Devil. I gasped and panted, grabbed hold of the urinal pipe, and held on for dear life as that man started sucking out a fresh bucket of cream, mouth-milking my joint like he'd eat me alive. I was really surprised when he pulled off just as my man-milk started erupting. He held my spurting cock in his fist and jacked the meat so the stream of cum arched and spewed into his wide-open mouth, giving the other guys a look. I pushed my hips out so far, it felt like I'd thrown my back out of joint as I shuddered and pumped the juice to him. Old Devil was spitting fire.

The man squatting beside me pumped his meat faster as he gulped down the cream. Suddenly, his cock went off, and shot long strings of his white stuff all over my boots. Then I really couldn't believe it when he pulled off the just-drained cock and started licking his own cum off the leather. Somebody said, "Whew!" and the party was all over. Then the man who'd sucked me off slipped a bill into my hand. Confused, I took it.

They all left and I went outside and sat on a park bench. Thinking again. Why would he give me money for pleasuring me? It was me that got off, better than any jackoff I'd ever had. I left it at thinking he was just being nice. Anyway, the rest of that day, I was as busy as a rooster with two peckers. I lost track of how many times I came in different men's mouths. All my previous years compressed into that one day, making up for lost time. I bought a hamburger in the same joint late in the afternoon and began wondering about a place to sleep. I went back to the park bench and watched the toilets. It got to be twilight and there weren't so many people around.

An old man went into the bathroom and came right back out. Then another younger guy with a moustache did the same. I figured it was empty, but decided to check. Old Devil wanted to go back to school again. I entered the pissy smelling toilets and saw no one at the urinals. Walking along the row of crappers, I came to the one I'd first used and saw a good-looking man in his early twenties, with curly black hair. His jeans were pushed down around his ankles, and he was stroking his dick. I went into the stall next to him and dropped my coveralls like a professional.

Peering through the hole, I saw him watching me. My hard-on was nudging against a wet spot above my navel. He grinned, and he was real cute. I started to stand up, but before I could, he stood and his cock came through the hole. It was red and glistening and clipped, clean and long.

I clasped it in my hand and heard him sigh from the other side. I figured I'd give him a handjob. I wasn't quite ready to suck my first dick—figured I'd get some more experience, see how the other guys did it.

But then he moaned softly, "Suck it, lick on it for me." Tentatively, I stuck out my tongue and licked the cockhead. He sighed more deeply. "Ah, yeah! That's it! Eat it, man, eat that cock!" His voice, low and gravelly, sexed me up all to hell.

I opened my mouth and put just my lips around the head, tasting his pre-cum which was mellow and very pleasant. The heat from his dick surprised me—it was hotter than my mouth. And his cockskin was so soft, so slippery on the bone of his hardness, it inflamed my sensitive lips. I pushed more of the meat-shaft into my mouth, till the fat dickhead was nudging the gag-trigger at the back of my throat. Oh God—this was true heaven; the best thing I'd ever tasted in my life. Now I understood why I'd been paid. I was an instant convert to cocksucking.

My animal nature took over and I rammed that dick down my throat like I'd been born to it and doing it all my life. I felt like I was gonna come again from just gnawing on my first taste of manmeat.

"Suck, man, suck!" the guy panted. "Make me come—I'm close!"

And he was; his cock was jerking in spasms inside my mouth and I had only a minute to wonder what my first taste of cum would be like. He started pounding his hips on the partition, slamming that cock in and out of my throat, grunting and groaning, then straining against the wall, pushing all out against it, shuddering and jerking his loins and grinding that cockhead all the way down my gullet. Then he gave a deep, long sigh, a quivering, spastic convulsion of his groin and the milk flooded my throat.

Sweet as honey, nectar of the gods, the greatest milk I'd ever tasted. I fisted my cock with one hand, grabbed his cock with the other and milked out his juice onto my tongue, so I could savor every spewing drop of his load. I held his throbbing fucker tight in my fist and felt the spasms in my palm like the wild and mad beating of my heart. Then I started going off, shooting jizz all up my bare chest all the way to my neck. I felt born-again, baptized into a new life by his cum. I loved it.

The young man pulled his cock back through the hole and hurriedly dressed. I snagged some paper off the roll and started cleaning off my chest. Then he came around and stood in front of me. I looked up and saw his hand reach into his pocket. My dopey grin started spreading until I saw him flash a badge and remove a pair of handcuffs.

"Get dressed," he muttered, not at all in a nice way. Then my heart felt like it was gonna explode in my chest.

I whimpered, "What's wrong?"

"You're under arrest," he gruffly stated, staring at my wilting dick. Then he spat, "Cocksucker!" like he was spitting shit out of his mouth.

Just at that moment, two more men walked into the bathroom and they had badges too. "Got one, huh, Tony?" the fatter of the two asked, smirking.

My brain fluttered and flopped in my skull like a chicken with its head chopped off. The two men led me out of there with my hands cuffed behind me. I cried like a kid, begging and pleading with them to let me go. No use. They took my hillbilly ass to the jail. There, I was fingerprinted, photographed, and strip-searched. Roughly. I didn't even get a hard-on. Through my tear-streaked eyes, I saw them write down, "Soliciting for sex. Lewd and lascivious conduct in public."

Soliciting! Hell, the fucker practically shoved his cock in my mouth! And the bastard let me blow him all the way to coming his nuts before he arrested me. It seemed so damned unfair, and my first cock at that.

They gave me an orange uniform to wear, like mechanic's coveralls, but with "Prisoner" written real big on the back. All this seemed to take hours. They ushered me through a series of iron-barred doors, and the sound of each one clanging shut behind me got me sobbing again. Then they turned me over to a skinny black guy whose name tag informed me that he was Cecil, the jailer. He got a big old grin on his face when he read the paper they handed him. I followed Cecil down a row of jail cells that smelt like piss and pine oil cleaner. A couple of guys whistled at me, and a few shouted remarks about cherry ass. I'd never been so scared in my life and hoped I wouldn't shit in the uniform.

The black guy stopped in front of a cell and fumbled with his keys a minute. Then, as he threw open the door, he said, "Got you some fresh white bread, Eustus." Then he guffawed so hard his spit hit me in the face.

"'Bout fucking time, Cecil," the man sitting on the lower of two bunk beds growled. "Daddy Five's overworked." Then he laughed wickedly. I heard more laughing from beyond us, but couldn't see through the concrete wall.

Truthfully, I couldn't see anything beyond the man sitting in front of me. For he was the blackest black man I'd ever beheld, and one of the biggest men you could imagine. His body would make two and a half of mine, shoulders alone, probably three. His face was round, and he was completely bald, large fleshy lips all purple and glistening, curled in a half-smile, eyes looking worldly and smart, like he knew everything there was to know about me. He didn't look malicious, more like he was chuckling inside, amused at my gaping expression. I didn't know who George Foreman was at the time, but later decided that Eustus was a near dead-ringer, only more black.

I took in the open steel toilet and stained porcelain sink, two folding chairs, and a little desk, after I dragged my eyes off of Eustus.

"Welcome to my nest, cracker boy," Eustus said after Cecil had gone off swinging his keys and humming. "What you called?"

"Jeremiah," I stammered. "Jeremiah Jebediah Samuels."

"Whew, boy," he said with a grin. "Folks call you Jerry?"

"No, sir," I said.

"No call to be sirring," he said. "Name's Eustus. We gonna be too close ta *sir*."

He got off his bunk and walked over to the toilet. Like I wasn't even there, he unbuttoned his orange uniform at the groin and hauled his meat out. Good God-a-mighty! It was the biggest fucker I'd ever seen. In a day of bewildering first-timers, that cock made all the rest seem smallish. The awesome thing had to be over a foot long, and fat. Just like Eustus himself, proportionately, with the fat dickhead all round and shiny-bald when he skinned it back, just like his head.

Eustus was standing sideways to me, making sure I saw every damned inch. He even stroked the fucker while looking straight into my astonished eyes. And when the horsecock piss started gushing out of his black hose, a ring of water splashed out and splattered on the floor. Eustus laughed. I heard a crazy giggling from across the way, and looked through the bars to the cell across from ours.

There was a ferret-faced white man in there alone, skinny and with a scraggly beard. He was standing at the bars playing with himself inside of his coveralls and he stuck his tongue real far out of his mouth and wagged it back and forth at me.

"Crazy muthafucka," Eustus said right next to my ear. "Gets off watching me piss."

Suddenly, the bare light bulb in our cell went dim, then out. Now there was no light except a gray kind of shadowy dusk which came from a tiny overhead light in the hall. I could hear men up and down the line muttering and rustling around in their cells. I couldn't see into the cells on either side of us, but from the side the bunks were against, I heard a low whisper drift through the bars at the front.

"Gonna fuck that honky ass, huh, Eustus." The voice had a black southern twang.

Eustus didn't answer, but I briefly wondered if screaming would do me any good; decided not, after what the jailer had said when he put me in there. By the dim gray light I saw Eustus shrug out of his prison garb. My breathing went to a shallow gasp and I stepped back as I made out the bulk of the man. Against the bars, his torso made a black hole to the gray, looking big enough to drive a truck through. I could see faint blue glints at his thighs. He was naked. The cell suddenly seemed to shrink, to draw close, pressing me tight to that nakedness. I started nervously backing toward the bunks.

He advanced on me. I could feel the heat from him and smell his male scent. "Now listen, boy," he said gutturally and low, like confiding a secret. "There's either gonna be blood on my fist, or spit on my dick—your call."

"You listen, Eustus, I can't. I ain't never done nothing like that."

"Time you started learnin' ta be a punk. I the best teacher here."

He started unbuttoning my uniform, his hands feeling meaty and huge against my bare chest.

"Fuck 'im, Eustus, fuck 'im," came that rasping drawl from around the wall.

"Shut the fuck up!" Eustus snarled. "Jack off, you muthafucka, and leave us alone."

"Make a lot of noise," the voice continued at the same low pitch. "Get that big ole black dick in that hole and make 'im squeal. Cornhole the little fucker."

"Never mind that asshole," Eustus said to me. "All we need is you and me and a little spit, baby." His hands were at my groin. In spite of everything, I felt my cock getting hard.

"Eat that ass," I heard a man sigh from the opposite side of the wall away from the solitary one. Then, "Suck my hole."

"Ole Bobby and Bernard," chuckled Eustus. "Loose bitches, tie a two-by-four on your ass ta keep from falling in."

"Can't we just jack off together—maybe I can suck your dick?" I pleaded as Eustus dragged the top of my uniform down and over my back, letting it fall to the floor.

"That too, little man," he said as he kneaded my asscheeks. His palms felt more like paws than human hands, nails long and raking through my assflesh, somehow tingling and not too bad. "We got time for everything."

I could feel his cock start to ride up, the heat of the swollen shank against my naked groin. He edged forward, pressing the head between my legs. Then he started truly swelling, pushing in further and his cockhead grazed the light tufts of hair on the insides of my thighs. Then I felt the shank creeping up to my balls. My nuts slumped over his shaft and pushed back between my legs as he poked more of his dark meat through. His wiry bush of pubic hair touched my lower belly.

"Lie down," Eustus whispered gruffly.

His arms were like steel cables as he maneuvered me toward his bunk. He pushed me backward onto it. My flesh made a slapping sound as I hit the sheets.

"Gonna fuck 'im now, gonna fuck 'im," came the muttering around the wall. "Fuck that white boy ass, Eustus, fuck that cracker ass." I could hear the black man's heavy breathing, seeming so close that he must have been crouched right against the wall. Then I heard the unmistakable sound of cockflesh being jacked off.

Eustus stood over me, his fat black club swaying, not all the way hard. I reached up and put one hand around the shaft. My fingers could not reach around its girth. The vein-filled meat jerked in my palm. I pulled up on it, and the loose dickskin dragged his shriveled black creambag up. I slid my other hand over the knob. His dickflesh was gathered tightly around the glans. I slipped my finger inside the heavy foreskin and found his peehole open and round and wet from drooling lube juice. Tentatively, I licked on the cockhead. Eustus held my head and jabbed his heavy fucker at my mouth. I opened my lips and he squashed into it, pushing the dickhead with two fingers between my lips. Just the bulbous crown alone filled my entire mouth as he managed to pull my lips over the blood engorged knob. I held the mound lodged in one cheek, filling it and swelling it outward.

Then Eustus took both hands off my head and skinned his cock back. It felt like something being born inside my mouth, a slow unsheathing of the swollen plum, swelling even further and becoming smoother, wetter. I felt the tiny nubbles of his excited organ on my tongue, pebbled flesh causing friction as he wedged more meat inside. There was no way any mortal could have taken much of the shaft, and Eustus seemed to be satisfied for me to hold the head and swab it with my tongue.

I figured if I could make him come, I might avoid the fuck. So I pushed his hands aside and put both of mine around his rod, and tried to suck as much dick as I could. Eustus began swaying his hips from side to side, up and down and around like you would move a screwdriver trying to gouge a larger hole in a wooden board. His cock-knob was wedged in back of my teeth, my lips locked onto it. His immense bull-balls hung low in their bag, swinging against my chin as he thrust his loins against my face.

From all around us, I heard soft moans and guttural sighs, sexflesh slapping, and an occasional piggish grunt. The heat was intense and sweat poured off my face and off Eustus's body as it slowly gyrated above me. The smell of his masculine musk was strong and heady, sex-charged and powerful. I began whacking on my cock, wet with pre-cum and sweat.

Eustus put his hands on his hips and stared down at me in the gloom, feeding me dick by hunching ever so slightly. Then suddenly, his hose threw a spastic jerk, a throbbing spasm, and started flooding my mouth with cream. He barely reacted, letting his cock drain off like he was pissing. He wasn't even breathing heavy or sighing, just spurting his jism. His cum gushed out like a faucet, and I barely had time to start swallowing, so unexpected was it. Then Eustus grabbed his shank and squeezed and more cum flushed out and filled my throat.

That brought me off and I shot all over myself. I grunted from deep in my throat, a strangled cry. Then I became aware of the sudden silence, a pregnant expectancy in the thick air around us, a listening void.

Eustus pulled his cock out of my mouth, and I let out a grateful sigh and took a deep breath. He pushed me roughly to the side of the bunk and stretched his bulk out next to mine. Taking my head in his hands, he cupped his huge lips to my ear.

"You'll do good, boy," he whispered wetly, his tongue slobbering the words in. "Real good."

"You feel better?" I whispered back.

"Getting there. You'll get two or three more loads, though—always come fast like that the first time." He took my hand and pushed it down on his cock. He was still hard, and the skin-curtain remained retracted. His tongue was fat and thick and wet as he slurred against my ear. "Turn over."

"Oh, Jesus, help me," I moaned, the most sincere prayer I'd ever uttered, and completely spontaneous.

"C'mon, Jerry," Eustus mumbled, turning me on my side and feeling all over my quivering asscheeks. "Gonna make you love this good black dick."

Was it rape? I guess so, because I would've never done it willingly. I thought I was all grown up, feeling so worldly in learning about mansex, drinking Eustus's cum without gagging. But I started crying again, pushing my head into the pillow and sobbing, trying to hold it in and not succeeding. Then I became conscious of that dreadful silence again, like the whole prison was holding its breath.

And then, Eustus seemed to go all different inside, started stroking my sides and nibbling on my neck, murmuring soft little sounds of comfort into my ear. He slid on top of my back and propelled me to my belly, his weight hard and heavy atop me. I felt every bunched muscle in his body as he pressed down on me.

"Way it is, boy, way it is," he whispered.

He twisted my head around and pulled my mouth onto his. I was as shocked as if he'd suddenly started praying himself. He was making love to me. His mouth was so big, his full lips covered my face from my nose to my chin. His long, dark tongue filled my mouth as completely as his cockhead, but he was kissing me. All that early roughness, and disregard for me other than as a body and hole, disappeared. I stopped crying and found myself responding.

There in the dark, hot prison cell, this huge, bald black man started breathing new life into me. His long, black bone was completely wedged in my crack, and he began gently gliding it through the wetness. I felt every vein as he pressed its length straight against me, the cockhead at my tailbone. Its stretching girth alone had my ass-ditch pried open. I flexed and unclenched my butthole, feeling the heat from his shaft on my ass-ring. I pushed my asshole open to feel more of him.

Eustus started biting the back of my neck, working down my spine, nibbling and teething each bone. He bit my asscheeks, harder and harder, each one in turn. And then he licked in my trench. When his tongue slithered inside my butthole, I nearly cried out with joy. He raked my ass with those long fingernails, not hard but firmly enough to make them quiver. Something in the slight pain inflamed me, and I opened wider for his stabbing tongue.

Eustus reached under my belly, lifted my butt, and grabbed my cock, the first time he'd touched it. Then he used those fingernails to drive me mad. Tenderly, but with force, he traced one nail up and down the tube, encircling my balls with the grating edge, between my legs and along the ridge of skin which led to my hole. He clamped my body to him between his feeding mouth and my cock and started jerking me off. He reamed into my hole and I started shooting spasms of cum.

Just at the moment that my discharge began erupting through his stoking fingers, he pulled his tongue out of my ass, and jackknifed his spine and stuck his cock in me. The shattering ejaculation was a counterpoint to the pain of his sudden intrusion. But it worked. As my cum gushed out and I trembled and shuddered in his arms, he got that monster dick all the way up my butthole in seconds flat. And it only hurt for that length of time.

Then he lay still, panting and breathing deeply, his chest against my back, bellowing evenly. He cradled my head in one arm and kept me held fast to his cock with the other jammed up between my legs.

"Good, boy, good, boy. Sweet ass, baby. Get that good—black—cock in you all the way. Take it, buddy. Take my fuck."

He began slightly moving on top of me, not thrusting but more like squirming his butt around and lodging himself good in my guts. It felt like his dick was pushing all my organs into my chest. It had been quiet for so long, I jerked when that voice from next door panted, "You in 'im, Eustus? Got that cock up his chute?"

"Ignore him," Eustus grunted under his breath. But then he said out loud, "I done fucked 'im and come. Jack off and go ta sleep, Butternut."

"Ah, shit!" I heard the man grunt. Then he groaned and puffed some and came, I guess. There was also some panting and grunting and wheezing from the other cell, coming sounds, and then it was still.

"Just you and me now, buddy," Eustus grunted in my ear. "That cock starting to feel good?"

"Yeah," I groaned lightly. "It does. Really good. Move around in me some more."

"Like this? And this," he hissed as he began the slow undulations of his lower back, thrusting in now and massaging my prostate with his cockhead. "Want you to feel good, baby. Wanna make you feel real good."

"Yeah! Yeah! Yeah!" I heaved, every jab at my trigger sending tremors of pleasure crashing through my middle and darting up my spine.

Eustus rocked on my back, grunting and sawing his cock in and out of my hole. Suddenly, he pulled me tighter to his groin and whispered huskily, "I'm gonna come again. Feel it!"

And I did feel it, felt his log pulsing and jerking inside me, spitting seed to my hole. "Ah, yeah! Ah, yeah!" I sighed as he exploded up my rump.

I could scarce believe that getting fucked could feel so good. But Eustus's cock buried in my butt and spewing juice felt like the natural order of things. He made me come again. I didn't think there was any cream left in my body, but my balls must've been working overtime, so great a quantity did Old Devil spit.

"Now it gets good, baby," Eustus moaned, draining his nuts. "Just us together, me inside of you, working us up slow. Relax and let me do the work." He turned me on my side, still plugged together and began making the most incredible kind of love imaginable. Every stroke, touch, feel, thrust, caress, and kiss was tender and gentle. He used his long fingernails on my nipples, pinching and raking them until they hardened. His palm felt like hot breath on my chest, so lightly did he explore me.

Then he rolled to his back, pulling my impaled ass on top of him. He used both hands to twist my body around until I was saddled up on his cock and facing him. He pulled me down onto his face, and we sucked tongue for ages. His cock didn't go down a hair, staying rigidly implanted up my chute, me squirming my ass slowly back and forth and gliding it in and out of my hole. My stiffer rode in the friction of his belly hair, and I felt like staying in that heaven forever.

Riding his pole, I fell in love with him. As corny as that sounds, nothing had quite prepared me for the exquisite sensations which washed over my entire body, shuddering and trembling from scalp to sole. These shivering tremors started as slowly warming ripples, then small lapping waves of pleasure, greater the more frenziedly we took and gave of each other. Then a surging riptide of boundless passion carried me to breathless heights I'd never imagined possible. My groin was on fire with need. Need to come. And come, and come. And come some more and get fucked to death. Needed to make Eustus fuck his brains out in me. Fuck me and fuck me and fuck me!

"Make me come, baby! Make me come!" Eustus panted. "Get it, boy, get it!" I felt the first jolting spasms of a turbulent ejaculation flaming between my legs.

"Oh, Jesus!" Eustus gasped. "This is the good one! Take my load, boy! Here it comes!"

He threw back his head and shuddered all over. His torso tensed up and trembled, hips thrust as high as he could and straining, me riding him like a bronco, throwing my head from side to side and caught up in the throes of a wracking seizure. He started pumping his jizz in my guts.

"Come, boy! Come!" he groaned loudly. "Shoot it, baby! Shoot it!"

Spasmodic jerkings of his buried cock erupted gushers of dick gravy up my bowels and I pumped my meat furiously. Two thick cock-shots splattered on his lips and he frenziedly tongued them down. Another burst of juice hit him squarely in the eyes and more cum slathered all the way to his hair.

Eustus fucked me two more times during the night. The next morning, he asked me if the cops had "Miranda'd you?" was how he put it. I told him I didn't understand, and he explained about my civil rights. He told me about the arraignment I would be facing later that day.

"You can get off if they didn't," he said.

"The cop I sucked off must have been too rattled to think about it," I told him.

"Well, there ya are then—tell the judge."

I was shaking when I appeared before the judge. "How do you plead?" he asked in a bored way.

"Guilty," I answered smartly. Cecil the jailer led me back to our cell.

KITO IN THE RAIN

❖ ❖ ❖

I had to lean my ass over the end of the pool table to get to Kito's swollen shaft. He held it up waiting for me with one hand—waving his immense dong—and looking down with an expectant expression on his darkly beautiful face.

Kito in the Rain

I had gone to Belize last month to escape the intemperate climate of a Minneapolis February, and to lick my wounds from a recent separation, a messy split from my lover of three years. I've been to most of the islands in the Caribbean, those to the east of what was once known as British Honduras—now Belize, which is notched into the coast of Central America just at the southern tip of Mexico. I'd become tired of those places of sun and surf, tourists and the traps built for them, sandy beaches spoiled by American hotel chains. I needed a break from all that and, as I am a travel agent and get reduced fares everywhere, I decided to try it. My modest income didn't stretch very far on the other islands.

Belize City, the capital (inappropriately named—it's more of a primitive village), is a bustling place composed of a population very disparate in its composition—Mexican, Mayan Indian, and the English, who granted its independence in 1982. The city is predominantly black, though that designation ranges in shade from café au lait to deepest ebony—the latter, my own particular preference.

There isn't much to do in Belize. The laid-back natives drink a lot. There is one bar, named The Southern Cross, which could be considered slightly gay, a rustic place with a tin roof, palm thatched over that, and open at the front, so it faces the street that curves along the harbor, just at the mouth of the Belize River.

A pretty decadent crowd patronizes the earth-floored place: some British poufs who have retired here, and some of the young native men whom they buy. I'm only thirty-two, so I haven't had to resort to that practice yet, though it's a nice thing to know that when I age a few more years, some of these good-looking boys will be available. But that's beside the point.

I had left my Victorian, wood-framed, weathered hotel, called The Mona Lisa, at about ten in the morning on my first day in Belize. I'd wandered around the primitive, dirt streets of the town, sight-seeing, checking out the half-naked and well-muscled men who sweated and labored with their rude carts at the central market—a smelly place, though not altogether unpleasant, as I rather like a musky, coltish smell to my men. The day had been bright and hot, the humidity stifling, and I was perspiring a great deal myself, when I made my way to The Southern Cross, remembering it with pleasure from the last time I'd been there, before I'd met my lover.

The place was just as I recalled it, still dirt-floored, with mismatched tables and odd chairs scattered randomly about before the rough-planked bar, and a pool table in the rear. Ray, the same young, English bartender, was present, dressed in a camouflage outfit, and attending to the liquid requirements of about a dozen people. A knot of three good-looking youths, all black, sat at a corner table. They were obviously hustling, surveying each new entrant and cruising the patrons who were already there, sitting strung out along the length of the horseshoe bar. I grabbed a stool and sat beside one supremely dark-skinned boy, whom I judged to be in his early twenties.

The young man nodded at me and I ordered a Pelican beer from Ray, hardly glancing at the bartender, so distracted was I by the handsome features of the lad. In that brief second of our acknowledgment of each other, I had time to appraise his beautifully wrought face: wide-set, brown eyes, which had a tantalizing gleam in their depths, a broad nose, and fleshy lips much the color of a well-ripened plum. I believe he may have had some Mayan blood in him, as his cheekbones were aquiline and pronounced. As soon as my frosty beer was delivered, I turned my full attention to the boy and introduced myself, all the while taking in his tantalizingly bare legs, spread wide in the rough denim cutoffs he wore.

"Kito," he responded.

I said, "Billy. Glad to meet you."

With that short sentence, my eyes dropped from his face and

across his lean torso, covered with the skimpiest fishnet half-shirt, so that his large, brown nipples were plainly visible beneath the sheer fabric. His flat belly, even in the sitting position, was concave to his deltoid planes, and the merest touch of wiry black hair sprang from the waistband of his shorts. I could see, beneath the worn and faded fabric that reached to mid-thigh, a long and thick piece of meat growing along his right leg, ending in a swollen-headed lump just short of exposure.

When I shook Kito's soft hand, his large palm engulfed my own much smaller one. He briefly gripped my hand hard, then relaxed his grasp, and left me holding his hand for a moment. I felt a delicious heat that was already getting to me. I allowed as to how the weather was nice.

Kito nodded, then said, "It's nice now, but look out there," pointing out the open front directly at the ocean.

I turned on my stool and followed the gaze of his dark-brown eyes and his lithe mahogany arm, and saw an advancing storm. In seconds, I felt the quickening wind, which was tossing the waters of the harbor against the low wall of concrete separating us from the bay. I could already smell the sheets of rain that were rapidly approaching, drawing a curtain across the horizon.

Several of the older patrons of the bar had noticed the storm as well, and quickly left, abandoning The Southern Cross to Kito and me, the three other youths, and two middle-aged men sitting together at the end of the bar, talking in low voices to Ray.

The palm trees along the shoreline began blowing in the wind, their fronds like rustling fingers, stretching landward. The rain suddenly hailed down in torrents and pummeled the tin roof, ran in streams from the thatched, open front, obscuring the ocean and the street.

I turned from the sight, as Kito's bare leg brushed against my khakis, pressed my knee a moment, and then relaxed against it. I returned the pressure, looked down at his crotch, and then up to his sweetly smiling face, perfect white teeth grinning mischievously at me, teasing me with what I'd seen. Stretched and laid out long against his dark-skinned thigh was his bulbous-headed cock, straining out the side of his shorts, actually pulsing out some dribbles of pre-cum. I caught my breath when he reached over, took my hand, and guided it beneath the bar to his immense cock.

Kito's huge, swollen cockhead was uncut and fleshy. Deep folds of purple flesh surmounted a plum-shaped crown that was reddened and nubbled, as I exposed it by slipping back the slippery flesh.

He leaned next to my ear and whispered, "I need it sucked. It's been a long time."

I looked around the bar, which had become dark from the tempest which blew outside. I saw Ray still talking to the two men at the end, ignoring us; behind them, the three youths were disinterestedly slouching in their seats, sipping their beers in a bored fashion.

Kito had reached over with his soft hand and was caressing my swelling groin, languidly trailing his fingers up and down each side of my own blood-engorged erection.

No power on earth could have stopped me from slipping silently from my stool and kneeling down, then burying my face in his crotch beneath the bar. I sucked and slobbered at the exposed length, and pushed his shorts up to get more of Kito's meaty tool in my drooling mouth. His cock had a bittersweet taste of sweat and pre-cum, and it was all I could do to get my feverish lips around his apple-sized crown.

Kito put both huge, black hands to the sides of my head and pulled me onto his distended shaft.

I ate and gobbled greedily as he face-fucked me, moved his ass to the edge of the stool, and pulled the legs of his shorts open wider to withdraw his tomato-sized balls. I hefted his weighty nuts with one hand, and pulled them down the length of his long ball-sac, hanging low beneath the stool.

I plopped his thick cock out of my mouth and licked my way down the pulsing, jerking slab of meat, down the dark, wide tube on its underside, down to his swinging nuts. I took each one in my gaping mouth and rolled them around with my tongue. I heard Kito groan above me, and then heard something else.

Above the din of the pounding rain, I heard a youthful voice throatily say, "Eat it man, eat that cock." I jerked my head up from my endeavors and looked around the legs of the stool. The tallest of the black youths was standing there with his legs splayed open, hunched forward with his dick out, stroking the tremendous thing with both hands. The other two stood just in back of him in imitation, all three watching me suck on Kito's cock. I rose shakily to my feet and found Ray peering and smiling over the bar, the other two men opposite the grinning boys—an appreciative audience of six. My face turned red. I wondered what I was getting myself into.

"Go ahead," Ray said, "but do him on the pool table so we've got a better view."

I looked questioningly at Kito and he gave me a smile that would have melted the heart of an Arctic glacier.

I looked out the open front where the rain continued to pour torrentially down, secluding the interior of the bar from the street. "What the hell," I said and laughed.

Ray came from behind the bar, and I followed Kito to the pool table, the three young men trailing after us. The two older fellows joined them in a circle, as Kito stripped off his shorts and shirt, lay on his back in naked splendor, and splayed his legs wide open. He was the most gorgeous man I'd ever seen—and big! His muscular legs straddled the pool table, hanging over its sides at the knees, his woolen hair resting on the upper rim. His flat belly was even flatter now, and his cock stretched to just above his navel, still dripping lubricant from his hidden cum-slit.

I shucked my khaki pants and kicked out of my Topsiders, threw off my oxford cloth shirt and dragged down my Calvins. My dick instantly sprang out and jutted up. I watched as the other boys began to strip out of their baggy clothes, the two men fumbled erections out of their flies, and Ray shrugged out of his jungle garb. I had to lean my ass over the end of the pool table to get to Kito's swollen shaft. He held it up waiting for me with one hand—waving his immense dong—and looking down with an expectant expression on his darkly beautiful face.

I climbed to it and started sucking, greedily gulping as much of Kito as my slobbering mouth could contain. I licked and tongued, laved and lathered the fleshy shaft of uncut cock, my eyes darting about as the onlookers jacked their own dicks. I was interrupted in my efforts, as the tallest of the young black men came behind me and began kneading the cheeks of my ass, exactly as I was doing to Kito's as I ate him. The other naked boy played with my asscheeks for a time and then knelt behind me and started eating out my asshole, really deep-tonguing me like I've always loved. His tongue seemed to be as long as one of the watching men's dicks, and he drove me into a feeding frenzy on Kito's pole.

I continued slurping and sucking, now so hot I drove Kito's whole sausage to the back of my throat, and gulped it so deep I gagged.

Kito moaned and twisted under me, and I felt the tongue at my butthole leave and slide wetly to my cock.

I was being sucked by the other handsome youth, then suddenly, my ass was being teased by still another. The second boy had taken the place of the first and was eating my ass while the first sucked me.

The two older men went to each side of the table, and Kito took both their stiffened dicks in his hands and jacked them.

The boy who had been eating me out stood up and put his huge cock at my bunghole, held it there, throbbing with pressure, until I opened wide for him, and he drove the huge shaft into my quivering hole. I groaned around Kito's pumping pipe, as the other hunched his way in, and ground my pelvis against the table.

The sucking boy beneath Kito had to reposition himself in order to take me straight down. The third youth advanced on the one fucking me and slid his cock up the fucker's ass. They worked in tandem on each flaming butt, and I felt like I was going to cream any minute.

Kito released one of the men's dicks he was jerking and motioned for Ray to come to his tilted head. Ray brought over his hard meat, and Kito started to suck him. I looked up and watched as Kito's gorgeous, thick black lips engulfed all of Ray's overlarge cock. The bartender was fucking himself into my beautiful Kito with thrusting strokes.

The boys in back of me pumped on in equal rhythm, sending waves of chilling vibrations up and down my spine. The boy in my ass clasped my hips and drove himself into my guts, while the other kid gobbled me below.

The two men at our sides were now gently caressing and kneading Kito's trembling body, pinching his tightened nipples and twisting his taut tits, one of them egging us on all the while.

"Oh, yeah, man, eat that good, black cock. Make him blow his nuts. Make him cream his jism deep in your throat. That's it. Take it, man. Take that juicy dick!"

They were pushing their hips into the edge of the pool table and Kito was jacking them faster, while still sucking Ray, who was pounding away with his grinding loins, facefucking Kito's drooling mouth and holding his head to his thrusting crotch.

There was sex smell in the humid air as the rain pounded outside. I knew I was going to shoot my wad any minute, but I wanted to get Kito's precious load first. So I held back as best I could, tried not to think of how good the sliding cock in my ass felt, and tried to think of something other than the gobbling, slurping boy working on my meat. My fucker's balls were slamming against my ass, while his reamer's slammed his. I could hear the slapping sounds, as they groaned and moaned and shoved their fucks into Kito and me.

I concentrated on the sliding, fleshy tool, its so-soft skin slipping up and down between my burning lips, tight against the hardness of coursing blood inside. I pulled off to take a breath and jacked Kito with both slimy hands, spat to make him slimier, and mounded his plum-shaped crown. I kissed at the soft, folded flesh, which was skinned back and hanging pendulously. With one hand, I twisted and kneaded Kito's balls, and he groaned blissfully around Ray's cock, deep inside his pulsing throat. I slipped both hands beneath Kito's trembling butt, feeling his twin globes like melons, dimpling as he flexed the heavy muscles in them. I put my right hand to my mouth and spat on my fingers again. I returned my attention to Kito's puckered ass, slipped one finger in, and worked it in and out, then did the same with two.

Kito ground down on them and his butthole opened further. I stuck in a third and fingerfucked him—and he spread his legs still wider.

The other man on our side slid his hands over our joined bodies, gliding his palms over all the streaming flesh as we humped and fucked and sucked in unison. He kept up a breathless monologue. "Like that cock in your ass, don't you, man? You want him to blow his nuts in you, don't you?"

"Oh, yeah!" I managed to get out, dribbling saliva down Kito's thick tool.

The man kept on encouraging me. "Go for it, guy. Eat him good. Swallow all that big, black cock. Take it up to the balls, man. Eat it. Eat that dick!"

I lunged deeper onto the thick-veined fuckstick, getting all of Kito inside my mouth again. The guy in back rammed faster; I sucked harder.

Kito flexed his hip muscles upward, driving his fuckpole down my distended throat.

I felt my balls churning with cum, rivers of electricity that shot from my ass to the base of my nuts. The grinding cock inside me was pumping me up to the ultimate limit. I was going to explode into the feeding cocksucker's mouth any minute. I couldn't hold back. I sucked faster.

Kito sucked Ray faster, too. The two men jacked and jerked at their cocks. My bursting dick was throbbing in and out of the sweet, hot, tight mouth that had a liplock on it.

The big guy at my ass was really shoving it to me now, pistoning away at my backside, pounding my butt with his hip bones, and the kid fucking him was matching his thrusts, stroke for stroke. We were all going for it now, going for the silver—the silver streams of jism.

The guy who was talking got it off first. His jism started to spurt from Kito's milking fist. His labored breathing became more ragged as he shot, saying, "Oh, yeah! Oh, yeah! Milk me, baby. I'm coming, I'm coming. Aghh!" He shot all over Kito's lithe torso, bursts of white cream spraying in arcs across Kito's molasses-colored body, coating and running in rivulets down his thin, smooth ribs.

His buddy got his nut just after, though not spraying far, but drooling a heavy flow of seed out of his boiling prick, and spilling in streams to Kito's belly. I ran my hands all over Kito's heaving form, smearing him with cum, giving him a new lining of silver semen.

The guy who was fucking my fucker shot off next. He threw his head back and groaned, "I'm shooting, man! Take that load, baby. Take it, take my scum!"

I felt as if he were shooting into me, so far did he drive his damned thing into the other guy. I heard him gasp over and over as he filled him with his wad of cum. I felt the guy in my asshole driving deeper, going for it all out, as he fucked me to heaven on a stairway of lust.

He gibbered and jerked atop me, balls slapping my ass, and plunging his meaty tool to the fullest length I'd ever been penetrated before. He hit my prostate and ground on it, his full-headed glans socking it with each harder and harder thrust.

I felt him start to flush himself inside of me, felt his cock rippling and jerking as he shot up my butt, filling my sore bunghole with creamy milk.

From the feel of the kid's mouth working on my cock, I knew he was jacking himself off between my legs. He must have been ready to unload too, because I felt him gasping around my meaty member, and felt the tension in his mouth increase as he gobbled harder at me. I felt his cum splattering on my bare calves, dripping over my ankles to the top of my feet.

I looked up at Ray and he was leaning back, his spine arched and pelvis thrust out, facefucking Kito and feeding him his dick. Kito was really lipstroking that thing, milking it with his fleshy lips, their pink cushions sliding up and down on the glistening, spit-slick cock.

Ray went into his orgasm with a fury, screaming at Kito, "Get it, man, get it. Get it, man, get it. Eat my cum!"

I felt Kito's own spasms of climax begin, the first pulsing stirrings roaring from deep within his tightening balls, rolling in their sacs like eggs in a pot of boiling water. I shoved my three fingers to the limit in his butt, twisted and fucked him with them, and felt his meat stiffen even more, the cockhead flare and swell inside my gullet, filling my deep-throated blowjob from side to side.

Kito started pumping his loins up and down, his ass pounding on the felt-covered table, fucking himself on my fingers and shoving his fuckpole into my siphoning mouth. I fed on it with a frenzy.

Ray shot into Kito then. I could feel his lusty explosion into the same body I was gnawing on, just as readily as I felt my own hot nuts start to spew out great gobbets of cum into the still working mouth of the boy beneath me.

That's when I got it from Kito. His huge cock erupted like a geyser inside my mouth. I'd pulled it to just the crown, so I could taste all of him, treasure his sweet cum filling me. The boy below milked me like my very essence and center were being drained from between my legs.

Kito kept spewing his cream, wad after wad of his nectared honey, his cock shooting load after load of man-seed into my hungry cavity.

I slurped and swallowed, slurped and swallowed some more, his bittersweet cum tasting like a nectar of the gods. My nose was filled with the smell of cum. My mouth was filled with the taste of cum. I had cum up my butt, all over my hands, all over my legs and feet. I had cum in my belly. I had cum on my face, on my lips and on my mind.

But if I had cum on my mind, I had something else, too. I had Kito there. I had the image of Kito engraved there.

As we all redressed, Kito with a dignity I was falling more in love with as each minute went by, I didn't know how to tell him what I felt. As we giddily resumed our seats at the bar, Ray passed out fresh beers all around.

The storm both within and outside the bar had receded, leaving only a drizzling mist. After we finished our beers, Kito rose and invited me to follow him with a subtle motion of his head. He and I walked in the rain and talked for the next two hours. There was no sense of awkwardness about Kito at all. He was a naturally sensate being, proud and reveling in his sexuality, as he walked with me and spoke softly in that husky whisper of his.

I invited Kito to come back to my hotel with me and he did. We made love several times each day during the next week of my vacation.

On my last night in Belize, at the end of a frantic fuck, Kito whispered, "Don't fear. We will be together again. You can return here on your next vacation and I will visit you. Who knows, perhaps I will like your weather in Minneapolis."

EBONY PEARLS

❖ ❖ ❖

Gary hefted the camera to his shoulder and made some adjustments while Russell started undressing me. When I was naked in front of them, Russell. . .was hard and lubing. Then Gary trained the lens on us and started directing.

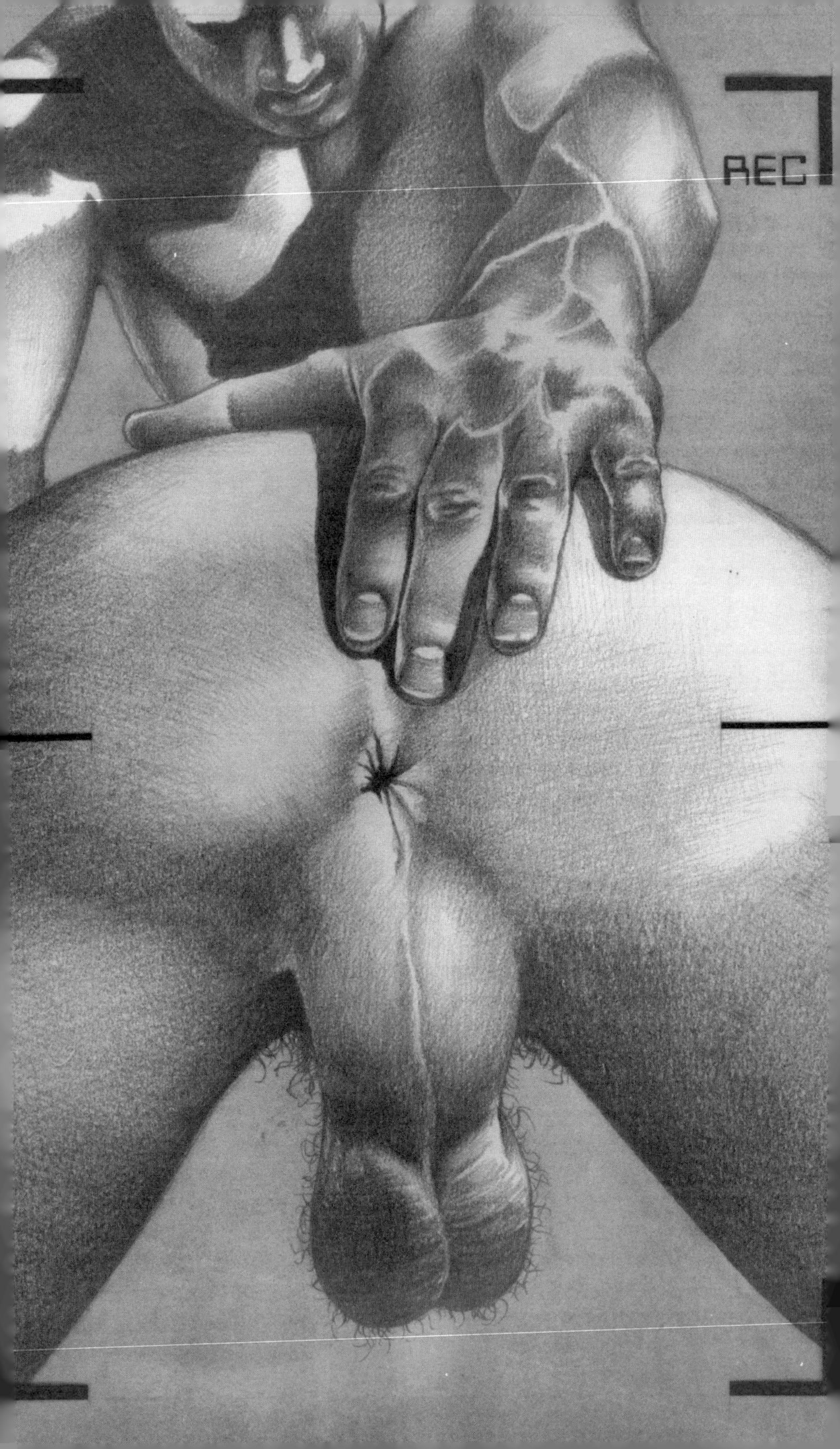
REC

EBONY PEARLS

"Damn, Johnny! I'm so horny I'd fuck a white boy," Russell hissed, jabbing me in the ribs at the waiter's station, and indicating my latest party with a nod of his head. This was Russell's eternal little joke since I'd gotten this job at one of New Orleans' finest restaurants. It was no secret that we would both fuck any color of boy. Russell is as black as soot, where I'm more café au lait. He's a couple of years older than my twenty-three. He's a round-faced, jovial guy whom I really like as a friend. Though he's big all over, he's rock-solid muscle.

"Not much chance of your black ass humping any of those white boys," I replied, nodding to a noisy group of college students down from LSU in Baton Rouge, out for a night on the town. They were mostly drunk and loutish, rude I'd thought, after taking their order.

"That one's a pretty boy, Johnny—kid with the long yellow hair at the end," Russell whispered.

"White-bread cracker," I sneered. He was the very one who'd been the most difficult, changing his order at least four times and then complaining about the steak being dry and tough after he'd ordered it well. I told Russell that as we stood there wrapping fresh silverware in thick linen napkins.

"Watcha doin' after work, Johnny?" Russell asked, dismissing the issue.

"Hit the bars, try to get laid—same old shit."

"You could come to my place," he said, slapping glasses of ice water on a tray for a new party who were being seated by the head waiter.

"We been over that, Russell—don't start," I said quarrelsomely.

He muttered something under his breath and left to wait on his customers. Trouble was, Russell was in love with me, or at least he thought he was, told me so all the time. We'd fucked around shortly after I met him, and he was a dynamite fuck, big-dicked and hard-muscled all over. But I didn't love him in the same way, and wasn't really ready to settle down with any one man. It wasn't because he was black. Being the product of an interracial marriage myself, it doesn't particularly matter to me which side you happened to come down on.

Personally, I think that's the whole answer to race relations: After two short generations of universal cross-breeding, there wouldn't be any difference in any of us. And guys like me usually inherit the best characteristics of both their parents. At least I've been told that about my looks. But let me get on.

It was close to one in the morning before we'd finished with our last customers and were counting our tips side by side. Russell had made forty dollars more than I had, and wanted to celebrate. "Let me buy you a drink, Johnny," he said. "Promise I won't get in the way or cramp your style." I agreed since we were closed the following day.

We headed for one of the gay bars away from the Bourbon Street tourist strip, and as usual, it was packed and swinging. The music was deafening, and it seemed the patrons were all knee-walking drunk, also as usual. There was no room at the bar, so we scrunched up against the wall at the back of the room. Beer cases were stacked for holding drinks and lounging against. Russell walked to the bar and ordered us both a Dewars and water, having to shout above the din.

As Russell jostled his way back through the crowd and the strobe lights flashed across his crotch, I couldn't help notice his fat cock swimming around in his pants like a big fish flopping under the fabric. I wasn't the only one who noticed, either. A fairly young man standing beside me stared intently at Russell's groin as my friend handed me my drink. I thanked Russell and we settled down to cruise the available men leaning against the Budweiser boxes.

It began to get more packed as the early morning crowd edged through the open French doors, local refugees who hadn't scored at the tourist bars. I found myself pressed back against the wall, Russell in front of me, and the interested man jammed into my side. I felt the man moving against me, his shoulders shifting. I casually looked down and saw his arm on the other side of me, reaching across his body and around to Russell's middle. Kind of pissed me off; he'd seen Russell handing me a drink, and it was obvious we were together. Or maybe I was envious.

His arm was moving back and forth, and Russell was staring straight ahead, letting the stranger feel up his meat. Aggravated, I sneaked my hand to Russell's left flank and firmly pushed his hips sideways and more in front of the man. Russell didn't turn around, but the man's left leg pressed against mine as he opened them further, pulling Russell's ass between them.

It was dark back there, and I had only a dim view of the still darker wall of bodies in front of us. But I was painfully aware of what was going on next to me. Russell was slowly rocking his hips, pressing back against the man beside me. The man fondled Russell's crotch, pulling him back onto his groin. He paid no attention to me. I could feel a hard-on growing down my leg.

Then the man leaned forward across Russell's shoulder and whispered something in his ear. Russell's hand clasped me on the knee and he turned around and softly said, "We're together." Then he squeezed my leg.

"Sorry," the man said, looking at me for the first time. "Couldn't resist feeling. God, what a hunk of meat!" In the darkness, I got the impression that the man was in his late twenties, with dark curly hair and an olive complexion, Italian-looking, handsome. But I thought his manners were atrocious.

"Be my guest," I said, staring at Russell for clues.

Russell nodded his head at me and I didn't exactly get it. Then Russell faced me, reached down to my crotch and groped my stiffening meat. I went to a full bone on the instant. Russell reached toward the man's crotch and clutched his meat in his hand, outlining the shank and cockhead in the khaki pants the man wore.

I saw that the man had gotten Russell to a full stiffer, his uncut cock protruding out his dress pants on one side. I knew Russell never wore any underwear, and it was big-boned obvious he wasn't wearing any now. He took one of the man's hands and one of mine and placed them on his lengthy hardness. I could feel his thick veins through the slick material. As if my other hand had a mind of its own, it snaked between the stranger's legs.

I was surprised as hell, because Russell had already taken the man's cock out of his pants and was slowly stroking on the slimed-up fucker. I felt over the circumcised cockhead and it was wet and hot. Russell wrapped my fingers around the shaft under his and stroked the bone. The guy was good-sized, fat, and hard as nails.

"What's your name, buddy?" Russell asked in that soft voice of his, pulling and pushing our hands back and forth on the man's root.

"Martin, Marty," the guy whispered huskily, his breath coming in short little puffs. "Wanna go to my hotel?"

"Both of us?" Russell asked.

"Yeah, sure. Whatever you say."

"Okay." Russell said. "Johnny, you game?"

I wasn't quite sure if I liked this Marty character or not, him being so forward and all, and I wasn't really that used to threeways. But Russell leaned over and whispered "please," loud enough for the man to hear him. Marty did have that fat cock, and I was turned on anyway, so I answered by squeezing Russell's hand on Marty's joint and saying, "Okay with me." The hotel was within walking distance, so we took off with him.

In Marty's hotel room, it became obvious the guy was a size queen, and was more entranced with the size of Russell's cock than my well-developed swimmer's build. Or maybe he just liked darker meat. Whatever the reason, he barely paid me any mind as we all undressed. When Russell was naked, Marty went down on the floor in front of his swinging club and started sucking on Russell's joint and softly keening. I was impressed because not many men can suck Russell off, but this guy could take most of the shank in his broad, fishlike mouth. Russell pulled him off after a few mouth-strokes had gotten him on a semi, and lay on his back on the bed. The man crouched down between his massive legs and again began feeding on his root. Russell dragged my naked body on top of his chest and pushed my ass down to his groin.

"Lick his ass," he ordered Marty.

Marty complied, and it felt good.

"Suck his balls," Russell growled.

Marty sucked my balls.

"Eat my cock and get it wet," Russell barked.

I felt Marty's lips move off my nuts and heard him sucking cock again. Russell pulled my face onto his and started kissing me wildly, his broad tongue filling my mouth with fleshy meat. Kissing Russell was like sticking your tongue into an electric socket, so talented was his mouth.

I couldn't breathe, so I came up for air. I looked back at Marty, jacking himself off and eating Russell's fuck tool. Russell cradled my head against his broad neck, stroking my wiry crown and pulling my body tightly to him. He was all hardness beneath me, his muscles tense and straining upward against me.

"I wanna fuck you, Johnny," he slurred into my ear, his tongue flat and wet against the side of my face. He acted like he was unaware of Marty down there gobbling dick. Russell moved his head to my other side and whispered the same moist words in my other ear. "I wanna fuck you, Johnny."

My cock was digging into his firm belly, and I swayed my hips, grinding my hard shaft down onto the delicious friction of his body hair. The sensitive tube quivered and jerked against his heated skin. Russell began gnawing on my neck, sucking and biting, making me hot all over, a radiant heat which spread in waves over my body from the slight pain of the bites.

Russell reached around us to his groin and dragged Marty off his meat. He pulled Marty's head between my cheeks again and pulled my butthole open for the man's tongue. Marty sank his mouth-meat in me and locked his lips on my ass-ring, tunneling into my chute.

When my ass was as wet as a thunderstorm, and my hole as open as a barn door, Russell barked out an order to Marty that startled me. "Lick that cockhead while it's going up 'im!" Somehow, being referred to in the third person was a turn-on for me, like I was a disembodied spirit of Russell's sex cravings, a cock, balls and now an asshole. And the way he ordered Marty to pleasure me was sort of a pay-back for the disinterest he'd shown earlier. But Russell's cock was Marty's god, so he held Russell's godlike cock at my hole and pushed it up inside my pucker with his mouth locked around as much of the shank as he could get between his lips.

"Oh, God!" I shuddered as I invariably did when Russell's fuck-tool first penetrated me. "Easy, Russ. Please. Go in me easy, slow."

Russell held my flanks tenderly and gently turned me back and forth, loosening me up as if he were screwing me onto his cock. His broad, flat knob wedged into the funnel of my chute and he was very skillful about knowing just when I could handle a bit more. Finally, with much grunting and straining, my ass rested on his pubic bone, his cockhead at home deep in my guts. Russell lifted my torso off him and pushed me back till I was riding on his cock.

"Suck his dick," he panted at Marty, dragging the man by the hair around to our sides.

Marty got his fish-lips around my root and went down on me all the way. Then Russell took his head and started jacking me off with his mouth, his fiery poker beginning to move around in my guts, like stirring a boiling pudding as he rocked his hips back and forth, and from side to side.

Every time Russell fucked me, it seemed to get better, and this was one of the best. I was still on my knees, gradually beginning to move on him, working his cock in my hole till it filled me completely. Then I slid my feet forward, bracing backward with my hands until my legs were straddled on each side of Russell's body, ass-clenching his cock in and out of me.

Marty fed on my root as I fucked myself in earnest on Russell's big, black stick of joy. I arched my spine backward, made a bow over his sawing groin, and pumped my cock into Marty's dripping lips. I almost felt sorry for the guy. Russell was using his head like a vacuum pump on my cock, not letting him breathe as he pushed his head all the way to my groin and held him hard to me, butting up his hips and squeezing my groin between them.

But Marty must have liked it, because he was madly jacking off, grunting piggishly around my shaft, and sucking more intensely. Then suddenly, he lunged off my cock with a strangled cry.

"Ah, shit! I'm going off!"

Agitatedly he crawled his knees closer to Russell's twisting torso and masturbated himself in a blur over his heaving chest and belly. His cum blasted out the cockhead and sluiced off on Russell's chest, slinging a rope of cum up and down his fur. A couple of blasts slathered across my legs, and the sight of the creamy milk on Russell's ebony skin started me shooting off.

Russell grabbed Marty's head in a vicious vise and clamped it back down on my spewing creamer. Marty gulped and gagged, but swallowed all my load as I cut loose with a massive gusher of spunk.

Russell went off in me. "Take it, baby! Take it!" he gasped, thrashing my body atop him like a rag doll, twisting and gyrating my ass with rolling fuck-thrusts up my butt. I bucked his cum out like a squirming animal, squatting and grinding dick up my hole.

Finally, Russell let Marty off my meat, and pushed him back to my ass. I felt him licking the cream off my buttcheeks where it frothed out of my tortured hole. The fucking sucker liked it; it was Russell's cum, communion from his dark god. Marty turned out to be nice enough, even asking us to come back before he left town.

"Kinda rough on the guy, weren't you, Russ?" I commented as we walked back to the bar. He didn't answer that but reached over and tousled my hair.

"You're something else, kid! I love you."

I didn't answer.

One night at work the next week, Russell called my attention to a man sitting alone at one of Russell's tables. He was a good-looking blond guy, youngish with a moustache and a butch brush cut, and bright green eyes that were almost the color of frozen peas.

"That's Gary, guy I met a couple weeks ago," Russell confided in an undertone. "He thinks you're cute as hell. Interested?"

"Hell, yes," I said without a second thought.

Gary looked like a slightly older version of that blond punk rock star, Johnny something or other. Russell said he'd take me around to the guy's apartment after we got off. Which he did. But instead of just pointing it out, he stood by me and pressed the bell. When the buzzer sounded, Russell pushed open the door and pulled me up the stairs.

Gary was waiting for me—for *us*—in just a pair of Calvin Kleins. Blond hair furred a T on his chest, descending to a fully packed mound inside his underwear, the pouch protruding on the side where his cock was folded down, the head prominent and bulbous. His belly was corrugated and his pecs were well defined, hard looking. Russell introduced us and we shook hands.

And that was all.

"Got everything set up back here," Gary said, more to Russell than myself. I looked blankly at Russell, and he gave me a smarmy grin, shit-eating I'd say if it wasn't impolite.

Russell kept his big paw on my butt as we followed Gary down a hall. In his bedroom, I saw he had a video camera on a tripod and lights on either side of a big king-sized bed. There was a monitor sitting on the dresser. Oh well, I thought, another threeway. Gary hefted the camera to his shoulder and made some adjustments while Russell started undressing me. When I was naked in front of them, Russell shrugged out of his penguin garb and his cock was hard and lubing. Then Gary trained the lens on us and started directing.

"I think we'll open with you eating his ass," he said to Russell. "Get in the middle of the bed and go to all fours, Johnny. I'll get a real close-up shot."

I compressed my lips and looked askance at Russell. He got a dumb-looking grin on his face and started pawing up my ass. I was on hard, and he guided me over to the bed by my dick. Then he pushed me onto it and dragged me up to my hands and knees. Russell squatted behind me and palmed my asscheeks open.

"Ah, yeah, good, man, good," Gary said as Russell took long tongue swipes up my buttcrack. Gary knelt beside the bed with the damned camera glued to his eye, starting to breathe heavily and focusing on Russell's face and my ass. "Eat that sweet ass, man," he huskily growled. "Juice up that hole."

And God, it did feel good! Russell folded his long tongue in the middle and shoved it inside me like a cock. I looked toward the monitor on the dresser and saw his mouth-meat glistening with saliva and assjuice, probing in and out of my hole. Then he put a liplock on my pucker and speared deep inside me, his mouth muscles working on my tailbone. Gary zoomed in for a close-up and my tongue-stuffed asshole filled the screen.

Gary rose up and knelt with one leg on the side of the bed, and I saw his meat was hard and pushing out the fabric of his underwear. "Beautiful, man, beautiful," he mumbled, licking his lips. "Eat that ass, eat it, man, eat it." Then he panned over our whole bodies as he backed away, palming his hard-on with one hand while keeping the camera on us with the other.

Russell came off my asshole and climbed over my back, his hard body sweaty in the heat of the floodlights. "God, but I love your hole, Johnny," he whispered wetly into my ear. He wedged his fat black sausage down and lengthwise in my crack, slid it slowly through the lubricated flesh. On the monitor, his fat bull-balls slumped over the glistening shank, hanging low between his legs, the fat purple head unskinning as he humped up and down between my trench.

"Show it, man, show it!" Gary encouraged. "Show me how long that fucker is. Ride it down his ass like that. Oh yeah! That's hot, man, real hot. Jerk your muscle, make the tube pump."

I felt Russell flexing his ass-muscles, grinding his cock hard against me. Entranced, I watched the screen where his huge slab of manmeat was darkly sheathed between my cheeks, pressing down against the lighter flesh of my ass. The sight made me even hotter.

Gary crouched at the foot of the bed, shooting up between Russell's legs when Russell clutched his club in his fist and probed at my hole with the dark, swollen head, now unskinned and looking dangerous. Gary had pulled his underwear down and was stroking his meat, a single strand of drool sliding down his chin.

"Open for me, baby," Russell grunted, swabbing my ass-ring and pressing in more firmly. "Open up for Daddy, baby. Give me that sweet ass."

Russell reached under me and held my cock down between my legs, so Gary could catch the leaking pre-cum which seeped out of my cockhead. He squeezed the shank, and I watched the juice run out in a string to the sheets.

I spread my knees as far apart as they would go and clenched my teeth against the pain. Russell held me fast about the belly as his big cock entered my pit. Then I forgot all about Gary watching us, taping the performance. Soon, Russell was welded to my ass, his meat pushing my organs into my chest, his knob massaging my trigger. Through slitted eyes, I watched the screen as his dark meat tore me a new asshole. I squeezed my butthole tight to his shaft and held the loose dickskin fast as his bone rode in and out of my chute inside the velvety black flesh. In and out, the skin sliding back, pushed in, glistening with assjuice, Russell breathing heavier as he pumped his cock to me.

"Fuck that ass! Fuck that ass!" Gary muttered loudly.

I was barely aware of him madly jacking off beside us. Then Russell took my head and directed my mouth onto Gary's cock. Gary held the camera on his shoulder, pointing down at Russell's slowly swaying hips and long pistoning root as the meat rode in and out of my bunghole. I sucked on Gary's cock and Russell set up a quicker rhythm on my butt, rocking atop my cheeks and gyrating his loins so his club swung and battered in the flesh-custard of my ass.

I became aware that Gary had started coming in my mouth, so I slammed his spewing fucker to the back of my throat and milked him off like a gobbling calf. He shuddered all over and the image on the screen tossed around. Russell went into a brutal, ass-slapping, ball-banging fuck, a delirious and rampaging animal on the loose. I gave myself over to his savage attack, and he mauled my guts without mercy.

Gary pulled his cock out of my mouth and kneeled backward on the bed, capturing all of Russell's maddened contortions on my rump.

"Pull out when you're ready to shoot!" he barked at Russell. "Wanna get a good cum-shot of that load."

"I don't—I don't—" Russell gasped, "—think I can!" He yelped, and I felt him start spurting inside me. That was all it took.

My cock went off like a garden hose, as Russell milked my juice with a flailing hand. Gary swiftly got my jerking organ in his sights, and I flushed out a monster load of jism. Russell had stiffened up all over, straining hard against me, shuddering and sweating and panting as he shot off bolt after bolt of his dick-gravy deep inside my rectum. It was fucking great!

Russell made me come three times that night, and we got some fantastic shots of his jizz streaming out all over my body, white ribbons on my dusky skin. He popped a rope of creamy pearls from his ebony shaft across my chest one time that would've made Liz Taylor proud. I didn't think I'd be able to walk normally for a week, so sore was my asshole.

I finally began to grow suspicious when Russell showed up on my doorstep one night when we were both off. This was shortly after the encounter with Gary. He had a little blond hustler boy in tow. "They're testing my apartment for termites," Russell said. "and I don't have a place to take Danny here. Can we use your room?"

I looked little Danny over as I nodded my head. He was a cute kid who looked barely eighteen, but I'd seen him carded before at the bar, so I knew he was legal. They came in and I indicated the bedroom. They went in and closed the door. Sitting there, I was jealous, thinking about that little hustler getting Russell's bad-ass fucking. I boned up big time hard.

About five minutes later, the bedroom door creaked open. A buck-naked Danny came out. He walked across the room and sat on my lap, his prick hard as steel and digging into his flat little belly. I looked back at the door he'd left ajar. It stayed empty.

Danny snuggled against me, pressing his head to my chest. "I can't take that dick," he mumbled softly. His body was slight and slender, yet firm. His skin was milky white as alabaster. I stroked his smooth young flesh, a dewy dampness on his skin and a sweet smell of soap about his hair.

"Did he eat you open good?" I asked, knowing that always helped me.

"Yes, and then tried to fuck me with it. No good—he's too big."

He felt into my crotch and stroked my cock. "Let me suck you while he fucks you," he sighed, so softly I could barely hear him.

I allowed myself to be coaxed into the room, and Russell smiled as Danny practically tore my clothes off. I piled into bed with Russell and he kneeled in front of me. His body was becoming as familiar to me as my own.

Even though Russell was paying for this boy, I was prepared to take charge of the situation. So I lay on my back and put my feet on Russell's shoulders, lifted my ass to his groin and greased him up with spit. Then I dragged naked Danny astraddle my face and sat his ass down on my mouth.

The little fucker's hole was dry as sand! Russell hadn't even tried to fuck him, much less eaten his ass. That scheming conniver had put the kid up to this. But I didn't have much time to think about it, because Russell's club penetrated my hole, and I was soon awash in the joys of fucking.

I held Danny's cock at the base and Russell started jacking him off while I ate into the rich softness of his assflesh. The kid tasted tart and sweetish at the same time, wildly wriggling his little butt on my face and squirming like a minnow between us.

Russell fucked into me with a demented vengeance, a pile driving ass-ripper of a fuck. Danny leaned forward and caught my wildly swinging cock in his mouth and suckled like a lamb. I thrashed and moaned, grunted and groaned, fucked and fucked and fucked.

Russell went off in me like an exploding cannon, a gut-wrenching ejaculation that seared my senses. Danny sucked the cream out of my flushing nuts in wild abandon as he shot off his teenage juice between our grinding flesh. Another fantastic finish to a most fantastic fuck! Russell paid Danny for his part in their seduction plot, and Danny laughed when I told him I'd figured it out from his dry ass.

A week later we were back at our bar, leaning on the beer cases at the rear. A man approached the two of us. "You boys like some action?" he asked. "I saw you leave with another dude a little while ago."

I looked him straight in the eye, placed my hand possessively over Russell's crotch and said in a smooth voice, "No thanks, we're together."

"I love you, Johnny," Russell said, covering my hand with his.

"I love you too, you big lug," I said. "Let's go home and fuck."

THE BLUE AND THE GRAY

❖ ❖ ❖

The regiment I was assigned to was marching out the following day, and I wore my new uniform down to a secret place in the bayou. This was a special place in my life just then, because of a slave boy named Butter.

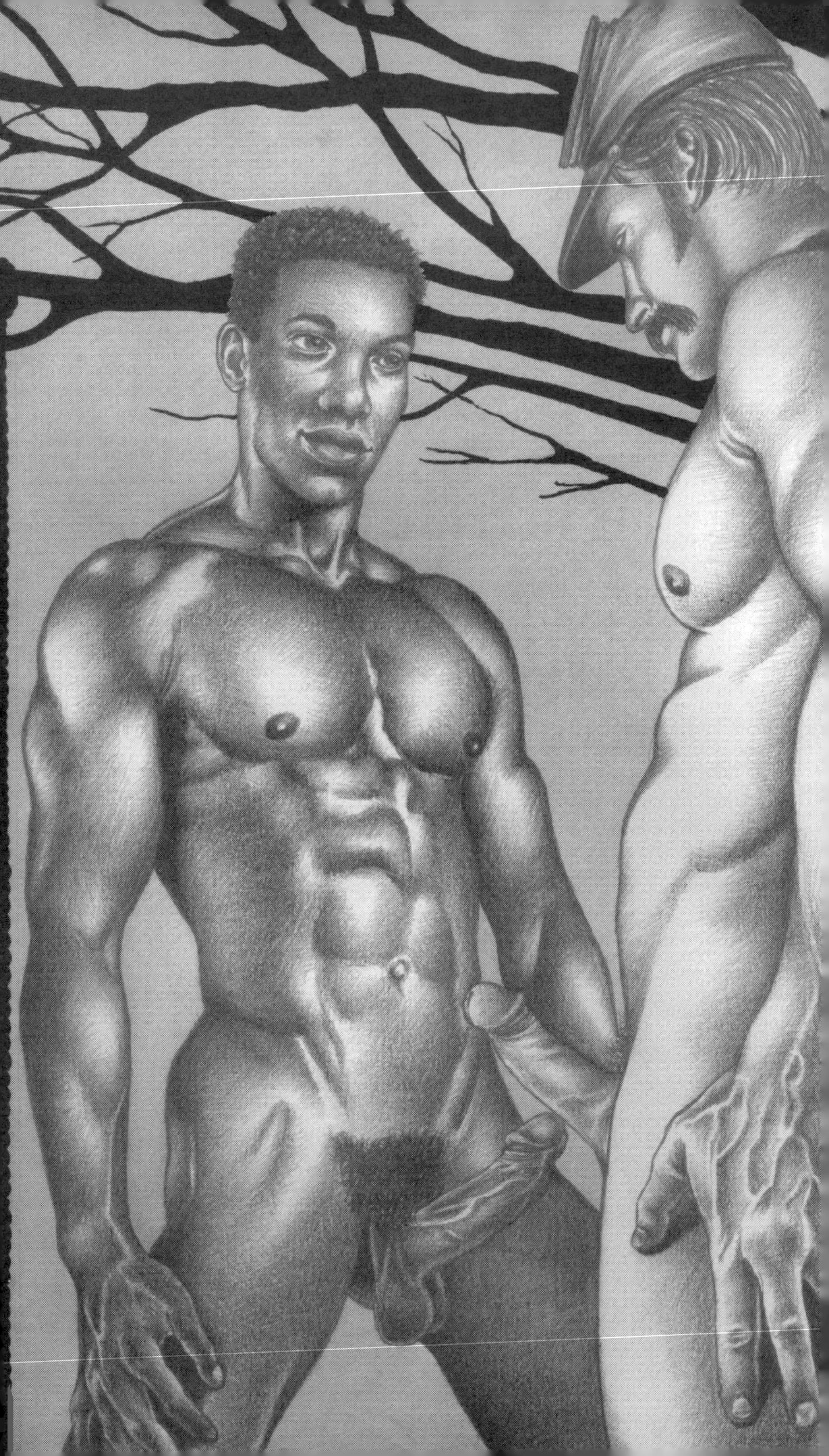

The Blue and the Gray

"Then I wish I was in Dix-ie, Hoo-ray! Hoo-ray!
In Dix-ie land I'll take my stand
To live and die in Dix-ie.
A-way, a-way , a-way down south in Dix-ie.
A-way, a-way , a-way down south in Dix-ie."

I was singing that song to myself as I traipsed home from the conscription office. I was mightily proud that day as I snuggled into my smart gray uniform of worsted wool. Truth, it was the finest and sharpest garment ever on my young body afore. And boots! Why, just as bright and polished as a gentleman's from the plantation, or like folks wore over in New Orleans where I'd been one time. And me never owning a pair afore, used to going barefoot.

I was a log cabin boy, you see, but hadn't quite done as well as Mister Lincoln, the gentleman responsible for all this mess, as my pappy called it. I didn't really understand too much about the problem that the Yankees had with our slaves. 'Course, I didn't understand too much about the problems some of our own folks had with their slaves. My pappy didn't own no slaves, us sharecropping our patch of cotton from a wealthy planter. And I'd wager I could pick cotton aside the best of them—done it all my life. My name is Andy Jackson, the same as General Stonewall's who died of pneumonia last year after the battle at Chancellorsville, but that's just a coincidence, though it made my pappy proud that I was named the same.

After things started going bad for the Confederacy up at Shiloh, President Davis lowered the conscript orders to seventeen, which caught me right unawares, being a year older than that. Hell, I didn't have no quarrel with Yankees, especially some Yankee boy I'd never set eyes on afore. 'Course I never saw anything in breeches I *didn't* like, Yankee or Rebel.

Everybody in Natchez was all excited about me going off to serve under General Hood. The regiment I was assigned to was marching out the following day, and I wore my new uniform down to a secret place in the bayou. This was a special place in my life just then, because of a boy named Butter.

Butter was a slave boy from the plantation which was down a ways from our neck of the woods, but I'd met him one afternoon while I was out trapping in the bayou that lies between us. I'd come around this big old cypress tree and there he was, leaning back against a tree, drawers pulled almost down to his ankles, no shirt on at all, big black cock out and jacking. He looked to be about my age. He didn't see me at first and I stood there awhile, boning up myself. The slave had big muscled arms and a powerful ass on him. His neck was thick and I could see the heavy tendons working as he gulped and panted. His belly was thin and flat, with ridges of hard muscles tapering up to a flaring chest, even more broad and strong looking. God, but he was a gorgeous sight!

He was turned sideways to me, and I watched as he pumped his huge purple dick while he stared down at himself with his long red tongue hanging out of his mouth like he wanted to suck himself off. I saw his ass muscles flexing and a near tortured expression came over his grimacing features. The boy mauled his swinging ball-sac with one beefy fist and fucked his hips into his furiously pumping hand.

I slipped behind a tree, untied my drawers and pushed them down over my crotch and ass and took a real good hold on my own heavy throbber. Lube juice oozed out of my piss-slit so much that I soon had it slimed all over my oval crown and slicked up my thick shaft. I started beating my meat and peering around the tree at him.

The slave stayed in his own private heaven of self-worship, occasionally skimming his palm over his heaving chest and twisting his dark brown nipples till they were thick and standing off his hairless chest like little hillocks. He jacked his cock like a sex-starved man, lusty like, and totally lost to the sensations he pounded from his groin.

He seemed almost like an animal in his rutting frenzy, and I was caught up in the lustful secrecy of the moment.

I knew I couldn't hold out much longer, but I tried to keep from coming because I really wanted to see the slave shoot his cum. Well, I didn't have long to wait. All of a sudden the boy punched out his hips and flailed away even harder on his meat. He threw back his head and bit his big lower lip, slitted his eyes, and groaned so loudly that I could hear his deep gasp from where I was hiding.

It was beautiful when his cock-honey started streaming out in long ropes, arching and spurting in thick, milky gushes. He bent near double then and shot off the last spewing gobs of glory onto his darkly handsome face. That fresh white cream on his smooth chocolate skin was the most beautiful sight I'd ever seen.

I unloaded my nuts when he licked the creamy stuff from his cum-slimed fingers. My running jism bolted up my thick tube and boiled out like a spurting cow's teats. The creamy cock-sauce slathered and sprayed the dried leaves at my feet.

And I made so much noise, he heard me. His eyes got wide and terrified. But then I moved a ways out from behind the tree and showed him my dribbling cock, still oozing cream, and he smiled right nice at me. Anyway, to make a long story short, I got to know him really good. And I fell in love with him. And I don't care what anybody says, Butter was the best and most beautiful slave in the world.

"I can't fuck a white boy," Butter had said, after we met a second, agreed-upon time. "Lynch me sure as God made little green apples."

But we fucked anyway. Oh Lord, did we fuck! That was the reason I wanted to meet him to say good-bye. Butter was already at our secret place when I got there. Together we'd built a little clapboard lean-to, and kept a blanket there for those times we slipped away and made love. 'Cause that's really what it was.

"Lordy, but you look fine, Andy," Butter said as I came around the myrtle bushes surrounding our hidey-hole. "Purt'near good enough to eat."

"You're the one I wanna eat," I said. "Just what Butter's made for—eating."

"C'mere," he said slyly, in that gentle way he had, those soft and warm brown eyes just melting me like his name. "Then eat me," he said in that delightfully wicked little way he had.

He licked his lower lip lasciviously and clutched his stiffening sex, tossing me a lecherous wink. He was kneeling up on the blanket and

I knelt down in front of him. His hand came down onto my shoulder. I covered it with mine. Then I let my other hand trail over the bulging mass of cockflesh in his trousers. I felt him hard and stiff as a cudgel through the soft, worn material. He reached down and caressed my chest, my neck, the back of my head. His hands felt like soft moths as they fluttered over my body. The wondrous magic of Butter's sex never left me. We kissed long and hard, tongues dueling and gnawing inside our mouths.

Pretty soon, Butter pulled my head down to his crotch. "Get on an' eat my cock," he said, pulling me over and pressing my face down onto his swollen member.

I never tired of the taste of his flesh. I pulled down his trousers and drawers. His big black balls were nestled between his legs and he lay back on the blanket and spread them open for me, reminding me of a frog with his pants bunched at his ankles. I licked and suckled at his secret sexflesh, nuzzling my face into his groin and reveling in the feel and smell of him. He reached down and guided his stiff prick into my mouth. He sighed as I sucked his cock inside.

I enjoyed sucking Butter off and jacking myself, timing my come with his. I pulled out my cock and dribbled saliva out of my prick-stuffed lips and into my hand and began greasily fisting off as I sank his warm, wet rod down my throat. I loved his wide, flat cock when it was hard, knew every pulsing vein on its broad shaft, and the bulbous mushroom knob from which I sucked off the curtain of skin and nibbled it between my lips. When I took him in all the way, as I did then, my lips were rewarded with the familiar tickle of Butter's wiry and soft pubic hair.

"Eat it, Andy, eat it!" Butter groaned, placing both his hands to each side of my working head. "Make me come, baby. Make me come."

I held his cock in the heated tunnel of my gullet and whipped my tongue back and forth on the throbbing underside tube, across which his dark veins sparked my palate. I lodged the fat knob against the backside of my gullet and milked it with rippling muscle contractions.

I hefted his hanging balls to my chin and sheathed it in the soft pouch of dark skin, reveling in the feel of his velvety sex flesh against my face, his fleshy sac drawn half over it. Then he began pumping his loins up and down, and I matched his frenzied thrusts with my bobbing head, my down to his up and reversed, again and again.

I brought myself up just to the edge of coming and held there, sucking hard and feeling the cum in my balls aching for release. I could probably come even if I wasn't touching myself; Butter's broad, black cock in my mouth was enough to bring me off. The tight tenseness of withholding my juices was a pleasure all its own. Then my rigid cock in my fist throbbed and released lubricating oil all over my grasp. Delighting in the joyous silk of my own flesh, hot and slippery on the bone of my hardness, I held fast and squeezed, pumped once, squeezed again, pumped once more, then held it hard, held it fast and still. Suck! Suck! Suck!

"Suck it, Andy! Suck that cock!" Butter panted, his hips pumping frantically up and down, propelling his juicy dick in and out my mouth, down my throat all the way, a savage driving need to come off in my mouth, his hands working my head like a pump handle on his dick.

Hung in that moment, I worked on him, his sextool as heavy as an ox tongue, and as alive and filled with blood. I devoured the lusciousness of Butter's hot sex as if it were the first time again. Again and again I consumed his taut muscle, the only one of a male you could milk.

"Ah shit! Oh fuck! Oh God!" Butter panted. "I'm fixin'ta come, Andy! Gimme your dick."

He grabbed my hips and twisted my body so my cock was at his face. Butter's lips were supple and soft and his mouth was wet and warm. The way he engulfed my prong, held it deeply sheathed, then lovingly stroked his way up, up till just the flaring crown remained implanted, tongued it, licked my piss-slit, and eased me in deeper again, quickly drove me over the edge.

When he stuck a finger up my asshole, I lost it. My cum flushed out of my nuts and flooded his mouth. Every burst of my jizz jolted my groin with jerking spasms. I unloaded my juice in spurting fountains down his throat.

I shoved my finger up his ass and massaged his trigger. He blew his wad of dick honey straightaway. Gulping and swallowing for all I was worth, I ate hungrily at his spewing load. Butter's spunk tasted sweet and salty at the same time, a delicious nectar of young manhood.

As we kissed, I could still taste traces of cum in our mouths. "I love you, Andy," Butter said.

"I love you too, Butter," I said. "And I'll be back as soon as this damned war's over."

I'd planned on asking his master if he'd see fittin' to let him go, or maybe ask could I buy him with the money the Confederate army was going to be paying me. We both cried as I took my leave.

"Man-y are the hearts that are wea-ry to-night,
Wish-ing for the war to cease,
Man-y are the hearts that are look-ing for the right
To see the dawn of peace.
Tent-ing to-night, tent-ing to-night,
Tent-ing on the old camp-ground."

Well, we sang that song sometimes, around our campfire at night. Almost a year had passed and sorely, mine was one of those hearts wishing for peace. This war was being fought by mostly boys, youngsters under twenty-one being the majority on both sides. And I had never seen such snow afore, freezing cold all the time, and hungry as well. My smart gray uniform was in tatters now, and my boots half-falling apart from all the marching. Our troops were driven back from the Potomac River and we retreated into the safe refuge of the Shenandoah Valley. Our casualties were awesome, and I was sick to my belly of the whole mess. Seeing these lads, some of whom I'd known as well as my own right hand, getting all blown apart with muzzle loaders, was the most awful thing I'd experienced.

Sometimes, there was a sort of truce between our two armies; them wanting the tobacco we had plenty of, and us trading that for coffee. One night during the summer, I was elected to cross the forward line under cover of dark and make just this sort of trade with the Yankees. My lieutenant gave me a little map with an X drawn at the spot I was supposed to meet the men who had the coffee. The Yankees were supposed to send two fellas to meet me at a place where three rivers joined between our opposing sides, and I was to sneak over there alone. I loaded up with about forty pounds of fine Virginia leaf in a croaker sack and struck off into the night.

Fortunately, the moon was full, and I didn't need any lantern to see my way through the sparse pine trees. But it was still a little spooky, what with night sounds in the woods, owls hooting and frogs croaking. I reached the banks of one of the rivers and followed it around a bend, where I'd seen on the map it joined the other two. Presently, through the trees, I could see the flickering of a campfire and figured this must be the place. I didn't want to just barge right into a camp of Union soldiers without first knowing they were the right ones, so I stealthily crept along under the trees, being careful to stay on the thick carpet of pine needles.

As I drew nearer, I could make out two young men in the blue tunics of the Union army. I'd never been this close to a Yankee afore, and suddenly got real nervous about it then. The boys, for like I said, that's all any of us really were, were sitting cross-legged on a blanket next to each other beside the little fire. They were facing me and sharing a jug of something, passing it back and forth. When one of them lolled his head back groggy-like, I figured right away it was moonshine.

As I crept closer, I saw that they were both half-drunk, with bloodshot eyes. So I took heart and boldly made my appearance before them. They didn't even try and lift their muskets as they eyed me blearily.

"I'm Andy Jackson," I stated. "You boys got coffee to trade?"

"Your poppa be the general?" the more muscular of the two slurred, having a difficult time focusing on my face.

"Naw, just got the same name," I replied.

I couldn't help admiring how good-looking he was: square-jawed and with broad shoulders, blond hair neatly combed where it showed under his pushed-back cap, blue eyes that were bright and sparkling with good humor. His companion was a smaller youth, with thin features, almost pretty the way his dark black hair curled out from under his cap in clean little ringlets. And their bright blue uniforms were clean and neatly pressed, tight creases straining across their knees which were almost touching. The brass buttons on their jackets gleamed and winked in the light from the fire. I felt more slovenly than ever in front of them.

"Have a pull?" the older boy asked, offering me the brown jug.

I nodded my head, dropped the parcel, and took it from him. I could almost imagine the taste of his lips as I took a swallow of the vile substance. I spluttered and choked and felt the potent liquid scalding my throat.

"I'm Eddy," the blond boy said. "This little feller's Mark." They were both chuckling at my discomfort. "You got tobacco?"

"Yep," I said and nodded my head.

"Le's see it. Don't wanna buy no oak leaves," Eddy said.

I dropped to my knees beside the croaker sack of tobacco. And the raggedy uniform at my crotch gave up the ghost. My pants split right down the seam and my underdrawers were hanging out. This threw the pair into a guffawing fit, laughing their asses off and slapping each other, pointing at my groin.

With all the dignity I could muster, I started manipulating my parts back inside the tattered shreds.

"Got some trouble with that big old Rebel cock, huh?" Eddy said as he grinned from ear to ear. "I hear you southern boys got big dicks—let's see."

That was true, at least in my case. Under their fervid stares, it was getting even bigger. And at that age, my teenage juices were always close to boiling over, especially with me touching myself.

"Yeah," I said, figuring to get some of my pride back. So I just pulled open the leg of my drawers and hauled that fucker out and showed it to them. My cock grew in my fist. I shafted it when Mark let out an appreciative whistle, and clear liquid drooled out of the fat knob. "Bigger'n any Yankee's," I said pridefully. I didn't know if all this was just childish play, or if maybe there wasn't something else going on.

Got my answer quick enough. Little Mark boned up. And something was swelling in Eddy's crotch. "Boys will be boys, no matter what color their uniforms are," I thought. With that in mind, I reached over and rubbed Eddy's groin. He was on hard and grinned even broader.

"Wanna fuck some Yankee ass," I said, stroking my hard-on lewdly.

"Mark's got the best ass in camp," Eddy said. "Show 'im, Mark."

The slim-hipped boy stood up and unloosed his trousers. His cock sprang out like he'd hit a trip wire. Mark's dick wasn't real big, but it was harder than the steel of my musket. Eddy pulled the back of Mark's pants down and ran his hand up the boy's crack.

"Real good ass!" he exclaimed, fumbling with the buttons of his own pants.

Eddy's cock, when he'd managed to slide down his pants and wrestle the fucker out, wasn't as big as mine, and I took some perverse delight in that. But still a good handle on him. Which I grabbed and stroked in time with my own.

"You wanna fuck 'im?" Eddy asked, turning Mark around and showing me one of the most perfect asses this side of the Mason-Dixon line. "Sweet, sweet ass."

"Ah, yeah!" Mark groaned as Eddy spat in his hand and greased up the slighter boy's asscrack.

I joined them on the blanket with what was left of my drawers twisted around my ankles. We didn't even bother to take our jackets off. Eddy lay down on his back and Mark climbed on top of him with his ass up and facing me. They commenced to kissing like they weren't any strangers to the act. I crawled between Eddy's legs and got my leaking cockhead up to Mark's hole. Then I drooled a string of spit down onto my dick and greased up.

A picture's worth a thousand words, and my prominent hipbones framed the gorgeous sight of my swollen cock as I slid the head inside of Mark's fiery ass-ring. He groaned loudly inside of Eddy's mouth. Eddy held onto him real tight as I worked more cock up his chute. The boy was tight, and his ass muscles gripped my shank with heat.

Eddy reached around and held my cock as its considerable length penetrated his buddy. Then he fondled my balls when I was lodged into him all the way, my knob butting against his trigger.

"Mark, suck me!" Eddy moaned. "Suck my cock with that Rebel dick up your little ass."

Mark came off Eddy's face and started working a trail of nibbles and sucks around his pubic area, tonguing on the cockhead he held upright only occasionally, teasing the larger boy and licking on his balls. Mark wriggled and worked his ass back and forth on my dick. I undulated my lower back and fed more meat up his hole.

Then Mark sucked Eddy's cock in earnest, going all the way down on the stiff pole and grinding his lips into the thick blond bush at the base. I fed my cock to his ass and Eddy's to his mouth. I held my cock fast and still within Mark's tender guts, feeling my pulse against the warmth of his yielding assflesh, as ripely churned as soft butter. He was about to make me come with his rippling ass muscles.

"Fuck 'im! Fuck 'im!" Eddy snarled. "Suck that cock, boy. Suck the cum outta me."

I began driving in a quicker tempo, hunching against Mark's warm backside and rutting my cock around in his hole by gyrating my pelvis against his sweat-slickened ass-globes. I reached around him and started madly jacking his cock.

"Make 'im come! Make me come!" Eddy gasped.

Mark panted and grunted around Eddy's cock, and I went at it harder, faster, pumping fuck strokes to his butt in a rapidly increasing fury.

"Fuck that ass! Fuck the cum outta him! Make me come!" Eddy growled lasciviously.

"Oh, God! Sweet fucking ass!" I panted.

"Fuck it! Fuck it!" Eddy yelled.

"I'm starting—to shoot!" I groaned, my breath ragged and labored.

"Slam that cock into him!"

"Oh, Jesus!"

Suddenly, Mark came off Eddy's cock and grunted, "Fuck it! Fuck my ass!"

"Holy shit!" Eddy barked. "I'm coming! Take my load, boy!"

Mark dove back onto Eddy's cock and greedily sucked him in all the way. He slobbered as loudly as the noise of our heavy breathing.

"Come, baby, come!" I screamed in Mark's ear as I jacked him faster. "Get it, boy, get it! Blow your nuts, now! Now!"

"Oh, God! Oh, fuck! Fuck! Fuck!" Eddy sighed.

"Yeah! Yeah! Yeah!" Me, strangling.

"Ah, yeah! I'm coming!" Eddy.

"Come, baby! Come! Shoot that load!" I growled to Mark, clinging onto him and humping my brains out.

"Fuck me! Fuck me! Fuck me!" he pulled off Eddy's log long enough to moan.

"Fuck! Fuck! Fuck!" Eddy yelped, wildly thrashing his head from side to side and pumping his hips up and down.

The spasms of my ejaculation started, racing up my embedded dick and causing me to shudder and quake under the force of the onslaught. I fucked into Mark with a demented fury, pistoning and driving my dick like a crazed pump handle in and out of his stretched hole.

I put all my weight into my groin and strained every muscle in my body, quaked and shivered as my cum burst all out and flooded Mark's hole. His cocksauce barreled off into my pumping fist, and the creamy milk shot all over the blanket and Eddy's legs, me wildly pumping his cock faster and faster, my hand a driving blur. The air was thick with the smell of jizz and sweat and sex.

I could tell Eddy was coming in Mark's mouth because he was puffing and grunting like a steam engine with every shot. Mark pulled off the spewing log and started milking the cream into his mouth in long ropes.

"Come in me! Come in me!" he panted while he gobbled eagerly on the spurting juice.

"Yeah! Ah, yeah! Coming in you, baby! Coming in you!"

"Work my cock! Jack that fucker—*off*!"

"Take it, baby! Take my load!" Eddy heaved out as he strained his thighs high in the air and Mark jacked his milk out.

"Yeeeaaahhh! Come in me, man! Come in me!" Mark slurred.

"Oh, shit!"

"Fuck!"

"Fuck!"

"Fucking shit!" I don't know who said any of that, but we were all like sex-starved beasts, fucking out our juice into and onto one another.

"Now we're all fuck brothers," Mark said mischievously.

Then my whole world tilted and seemed crazy to me. I might be shooting at these two boys the next day. They might even kill me. So I felt real peculiar as we made the swap, kissed one another, and I snuck back to the Confederate line.

Rumors about General Sherman's march to the sea, the burning of Atlanta, and the destruction he wrought, began to filter into camp. The final straw that made me a skeedaddler, (what we called deserters), joining up with Mark and Eddy in the Union army, was when I got a letter from my pappy.

He wrote about how a runaway slave was caught and lynched right in the middle of Natchez. The slave's name was Butter. I'm singing a new song now.

"Mine eyes have seen the glor-y of the com-ing of the Lord,
He has sound-ed forth the trump-et that shall nev-er call re-treat;
He is sift-ing out the hearts of men be-fore his judge-ment seat;
Oh! be swift my soul to ans-wer him, be ju-bi-lant my feet.
His truth is march-ing on.
Glo-ry, glo-ry, hal-la-leu-ja, His truth is march-ing on!"